POULTRY & GAME

by Anne Tynte

CONTENTS

Photography by Angel Studio
Copyright © 1972 Robert Yeatman Ltd. All rights reserved
Published by Purnell, London
Made and Printed in Great Britain by Purnell & Sons Ltd.,
Paulton (Somerset) and London
SBN 361 02198 4

TURKEY: FOR FESTIVE OCCASIONS

Turkeys are usually roasted for Christmas or other special celebration meals with a variety of stuffings, of which four interesting and delicious examples are given below.

When selecting turkey it is advisable to allow 1 pound of turkey per person (cleaned weight). This will leave enough turkey after the feast to eat cold or to make up on the second day.

The quantities given in the stuffing recipes are worked out for a bird weighing 8–9 pounds which will feed 8–10 people. If a smaller or larger bird is to be cooked, a general rule is to allow approximately 1 teacup of stuffing per pound of bird.

If using a frozen bird give ample time to defrost; otherwise the breast will be dry and over-cooked before the legs are done. It is advisable to use either the slow method or the French roasting method for cooking a frozen bird as this helps to make it more tender and succulent. The French method is also advisable if a turkey is being cooked for eating cold rather than hot.

If roasting a turkey without stuffing the cooking time can be reduced by about 5 minutes per pound.

QUICK METHOD
Turkey weighing 6–12 pounds, allow 15 minutes per pound and 15 minutes over.

Turkey weighing 12 pounds and over, allow 10–12 minutes per pound and 10 minutes over.

Pre-heat oven to 450°F Mark 8

SLOW METHOD
Turkey weighing 6–12 pounds, allow 20 minutes per pound and 20 minutes over.

Turkey weighing 12 pounds and over, allow 16 minutes per pound and 20–30 minutes over.

Pre-heat oven to 325°F Mark 3

FRENCH ROAST METHOD
Turkey weighing 6–12 pounds, allow 20 minutes per pound and 20 minutes over.

Turkey weighing 12 pounds and over, allow 15 minutes per pound.

Pre-heat oven to 350°F Mark 4

Traditional Quick Roast Turkey

For use with a fresh tender turkey which is not too large and has not been frozen (Serves 8–10)

1. Wash turkey inside and out with cold water. Dry thoroughly with paper towel. Rub surface all over with a cut lemon to keep flesh white. Fill the body cavity with sausage meat stuffing and the neck with chestnut stuffing, or if using other stuffings fill the neck first, not too tightly, and put remaining stuffing inside the body. *(cont.)*

1 fresh turkey unfrozen, weight 8—9
    pounds when plucked and cleaned
6—8 teacups stuffing
1 onion
3—4 oz butter
salt, ground pepper and poultry
    seasoning
8—10 strips fat bacon
6 tablespoons oil
10—20 potatoes according to size
½—¾ pints stock

Pre-heat oven to 450°F Mark 8

1. Use wing tips to help hold neck skin in place under bird and sew down the neck skin to keep stuffing in place. Close the cavity as tightly as possible and put an onion at entrance and tie or sew the leg bones together to keep it closed as much as possible. Rub breast and legs thickly with butter and seasoning, cover with strips of fat bacon and tie these in place. Weigh bird and calculate roasting time using table provided on page 2.

2. Heat 6 tablespoons oil in roasting pan. When hot, put in bird and baste thoroughly. Place a large piece of foil over top and roast for 2½—2¾ hours, basting every 20 minutes and turning bird from one side to the other every 20 minutes to allow legs to cook without overcooking breast. For last 30 minutes place bird breast up and remove foil covering to brown breast.

3. Test if bird is done by running skewer into thickest part of leg. If juice is pink, cook longer; if clear, bird is done. Another indication is when the meat on the legs shrinks back on bones.

4. Par-boiled potatoes can be roasted around turkey during last hour of cooking or in a separate pan in same oven.

5. Remove from roasting pan and put on large serving dish. Keep warm. Pour off fat from pan. Add 1—2 teaspoons flour to juices in pan. Pour on stock. Bring to the boil, stirring constantly. When well-flavoured, skim off any fat that has risen to surface and pour gravy into sauce boat to serve with turkey.

Roast Turkey: Slow Method

1. Prepare and stuff bird as for quick roasting. Weigh and calculate time using table on page 2. Do not cover bird with foil as this will make it soggy. Baste and turn turkey every 20—30 minutes, removing bacon for last 30 minutes and increasing heat to 375°F Mark 5 to brown.

Pre-heat oven to 325°F Mark 3

2. Make gravy using drippings from roasting meat and giblet stock.

Oyster Stuffing

1 pint oysters in own liquid
12—15 oz fresh breadcrumbs
8 oz butter
2 chopped mild onions
3—4 stalks sliced celery
3 tablespoons parsley chopped
juice of ½ lemon
a little white wine or stock

1. Prepare (or buy ready prepared) oysters in their own salty juice. Prepare breadcrumbs made with two-day old loaf. Melt butter and cook onions and celery until soft and light golden brown.

2. Add to breadcrumbs, with chopped herbs and seasoning, lemon juice and the oysters cut in half if large. If too dry, a little white wine or stock may be added, but it must not be too soft. Fill turkey cavity and sew up carefully.

Cornbread, Corn and Mushroom Stuffing

6—7 oz cornbread
6—7 oz fresh white breadcrumbs
4—5 oz whole kernel sweetcorn
4 oz mushrooms
6 oz butter
salt, pepper and a pinch of cayenne pepper
2 tablespoons mixed herbs chopped
2 beaten eggs
5—6 tablespoons stock

1. Crumble cornbread, add breadcrumbs, corn and mushrooms, cooked for few minutes in butter. Cornbread is not readily available in the U.K., so the amount of plain crumbs can be altered and more sweetcorn used 10—12 oz white breadcrumbs with 6 oz whole kernel sweetcorn.

2. Add plenty of seasoning, chopped herbs, beaten eggs and enough stock to make a moist but not runny mixture. Fill this mixture into cavity of bird and sew up opening.

Sausage Meat Stuffing

1 pound pork sausage meat
4—6 stalks celery chopped
1 large or two medium onions
2 oz butter
1 turkey liver
6 oz breadcrumbs
2—3 tablespoons parsley and thyme chopped
1 egg
juice of ½ lemon

1. Put sausage meat in a bowl with chopped celery. Melt butter and fry finely chopped onion and turkey liver for 2—3 minutes. Remove, allow to cool slightly.

2. Then cut into small pieces and mix into sausage meat. Add chopped herbs and breadcrumbs. Add a beaten egg to moisten, and a little lemon juice, and stuff inside turkey. Sew up opening carefully.

Hunter's Turkey (see p. 8)

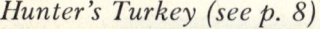

French Roast Turkey

Turkey stuffed with any of suggested stuffings or with butter, onion or parsley, roasted with stock to produce tender, moist result. Particularly suited for cooking frozen turkey or turkey to be eaten cold (Serves 8–10)

1 turkey 8–9 pounds
½ lemon
3 onions
6–8 oz butter
salt, ground pepper and poultry
    seasoning
a few sprigs parsley
giblets
a little mixed herbs
1–1½ teaspoons flour
turkey liver

Pre-heat oven to 350°F Mark 4

1. Wash and dry turkey thoroughly. Rub surface with cut lemon to keep flesh white. Put half the butter inside with 2 peeled onions and several sprigs of parsley and some seasoning, or stuff turkey with one of chosen stuffings and sew in carefully. Weigh turkey and calculate cooking time using chart provided (see above).

2. Rub remaining butter all over breast and legs, season and cover with foil. Put in roasting pan and pour around ½ pint stock made with giblets, 1 onion and herbs.

3. Put into oven and roast for calculated time removing foil every 20 minutes and turning bird from side to side to cook legs. Baste each time with stock, adding more if it seems to be evaporating too quickly. During last half hour place bird breast up and allow to brown. It may be necessary to put oven up to 400°F Mark 6 for last 10 minutes. Test to see if bird is cooked thoroughly by sticking skewer into thickest part of leg. If juice runs pink, further cooking is required; if clear, it is done.

4. Remove turkey to serving dish and make gravy. Skim some of butter from roasting pan and put into a small pan. Fry turkey liver until tender. Sprinkle in flour; then add skimmed pan drippings, plus remaining stock. Bring to the boil and simmer. Add seasoning to taste, and serve.

Chestnut Stuffing

Stuffing to go in neck cavity of turkey

1. If using raw chestnuts cut a slit in each nut and bake in oven in dish of salt until skins come off cleanly, about 20 minutes, or bring to the boil and cook for 5 minutes until skins are loose. Then remove all outer and inner skins, and cook chestnuts in milk or stock until tender. Drain and mash or crush in liquidizer, reserving a few to chop roughly.

2. Melt butter and cook onion until tender. After a few minutes, add chopped bacon and cook. Stir into chestnut puree, add salt and pepper and as much milk or stock as is needed to make an easily moulded stuffing. Do not make too wet. Add roughly chopped chestnuts last. Put this mixture into neck of bird and sew up skin under back of bird or skewer securely using wing tips to help hold in stuffing.

(Tinned fresh pureed chestnuts can be used for this stuffing but will need more onion and seasoning if the stuffing is not to be rather dull in flavour. Moisten with strongly flavoured stock.)

1½ pounds raw chestnuts in shells, 1 pound when peeled (or large tin of unsweetened chestnut puree)
½—¾ pint milk or well flavoured stock
1—2 oz butter
1 large onion
2—3 rashers streaky bacon

Italian Roast Turkey

Turkey stuffed with unusual mixture of prunes, chestnuts, sausage meat, pears, white wine and liver, braised in a garlic and herb flavoured sauce, and then roasted (Serves 8—10, hot)

1. Prepare stuffing: Soak and cook prunes in tea. Remove stones when tender, chop roughly. If using fresh chestnuts, cook in boiling water for 5 minutes, then remove outer and inner skins. Cook for 30 minutes in stock, drain and chop roughly. Mix these ingredients with sausage meat. Melt butter and fry turkey liver and onion for 3—4 minutes. Allow to cool, then chop and add to other ingredients. Add seasoning and wine. Stir whole mixture over heat for few minutes until thoroughly blended and hot. Let cool before stuffing turkey.

2. When turkey is stuffed and sewn up, melt butter in flameproof casserole and cook sliced onion, sliced carrot, chopped celery and diced bacon for few minutes. Add garlic, rosemary, peppercorns, and other seasoning and herbs. Place turkey on top of this, pour over ½ bottle red wine and enough stock to come half way up bird. Cover casserole with lid and braise turkey for 3½ hours turning from side to side every half hour to allow all sides to cook equally.

3. Remove from casserole and drain from sauce. Heat some oil and ½ oz butter in a roasting pan, put in turkey and baste. Roast in oven for ½ hour, until the bird has browned and is well done, basting every 10 minutes.

4. Remove garlic cloves. Boil up pan drippings and vegetables to reduce slightly. Strain and serve as sauce.

1 turkey weighing 8—9 pounds (if frozen allow ample time to defrost)
STUFFING

2—3 oz raw prunes
1 pound peeled chestnuts (or 1 large tin unsweetened chestnuts)
8—10 oz sausage meat
1 large onion
1—2 oz butter
1 turkey liver
2 liquid oz white wine (or Italian vermouth)

FOR BRAISING
1½—2 oz butter
2 onions
2 carrots
4—6 stalks celery
3 rashers bacon
2 cloves garlic
1 spray fresh rosemary (or 2 teaspoons dried)
8 peppercorns
parsley, thyme and 2 bay leaves
½ bottle red wine
½—¾ pint stock

FOR ROASTING
3—4 tablespoons oil
½ oz butter

Pre-heat oven to 325°F Mark 3

TURKEY: FOR OTHER OCCASIONS

Hunter's Turkey

2 turkey legs cut into 4 joints or 8
   slices turkey
2–3 tablespoons oil
1 onion
1 clove garlic
¾–1 oz flour
2–3 tablespoons tomato puree
2 liquid oz white wine
½ pint brown stock
6–8 mushrooms
1 oz butter
1 tablespoon parsley chopped
¼ teaspoon oregano
1–2 oz grated cheddar cheese
2 tablespoons breadcrumbs

Pre-heat oven to 350°F Mark 4
Pre-heat grill

Cooked turkey meat in a rich garlic, herb and tomato flavoured wine sauce, finished with cheese (Serves 4–6, hot—see picture, p. 5)

1. Make hunter's sauce: Heat oil and cook chopped onion and crushed garlic until golden brown. Sprinkle in flour, cook for 1 minute to brown lightly. Add tomato puree, wine and stock. Bring to the boil, stirring frequently. Add sliced mushrooms, cooked for few minutes in butter. Add herbs and seasoning, and simmer for few minutes.

2. Joint turkey legs or cut breast into slices, and place in a fireproof dish. Spoon over the sauce.

3. Put in oven for 15 minutes. Then sprinkle top with cheese and breadcrumbs, and put under grill to brown.

English Boiled Turkey

1 small turkey weighing 6 pounds
6–8 oz lean minced veal
3–4 oz lean minced ham
2½–3 oz butter
1½–2 oz mushrooms
1½ oz white breadcrumbs
a little milk
2 tablespoons chopped parsley and
   thyme
½ onion chopped or 1 teaspoon onion
   powder
1 egg
4–5 onions
3–4 carrots sliced
3–4 stalks celery
8–9 peppercorns
2–3 bouillon cubes
1½ oz flour
4 liquid oz wine
¾ oz gelatine (if serving cold)

Turkey stuffed with veal, ham and bread forcemeat, flavoured with mushrooms and herbs, boiled in stock and served in a white sauce; also excellent cold when white sauce has gelatine added (Serves 6–8, hot or cold)

1. First prepare forcemeat or stuffing: Mince lean veal and ham finely. Melt 1 oz butter and cook mushrooms for 5–6 minutes. Allow to cool before adding to the meat. Soak breadcrumbs in milk for 15 minutes; then squeeze out as much milk as possible. Add this to meats with chopped mushrooms, herbs and seasoning and chopped onion or onion powder. Beat together until very smooth.

2. Stuff cleaned turkey with mixture. Sew up opening carefully to prevent forcemeat escaping during boiling. If a large piece of muslin is available wrap bird in this and tie securely.

3. Put into a pan of cold water which just covers bird, with onions, sliced carrots, sliced celery, peppercorns, and bouillon cubes. Bring water slowly to the boil. Then cook slowly, allowing 30 minutes per pound.

4. Remove from cooking liquid and test for tenderness. Strain stock and boil to reduce quantity. Melt 1½ oz butter and add 1½ oz flour. Pour on 1 pint of the stock and white wine. Blend carefully. Bring to the boil, and when smooth and cooked, spoon over turkey and serve hot.

5. If serving cold, add ½–¾ oz gelatine to sauce and dissolve before allowing to cool. When cool, spoon over turkey and leave to set.

Deviled Turkey Legs

2 large cooked turkey legs cut in half
3—4 tablespoons oil or 2 oz butter
juice of ½ onion
juice of 1 crushed clove garlic
1 tablespoon tomato ketchup
1 tablespoon mushroom ketchup
2 tablespoons Worcestershire sauce
1 level teaspoon English mustard
1 rounded teaspoon French mustard
1 teaspoon sugar
a small pinch cayenne pepper
salt, pepper
4 tomatoes
12 oz rice
½ small tin tomatoes
¼ pint turkey stock

Pre-heat grill

Cooked turkey legs marinated in a devil mixture, then fried and served with rice and tomato devil sauce (Serves 4, hot)

1. Make devil mixture: Mix oil or melted butter with onion and crushed garlic juices, tomato and mushroom ketchup, Worcestershire sauce, mustards, sugar, cayenne pepper, salt and black pepper.

2. Disjoint each turkey leg. With a sharp knife cut shallow gashes into meat. Put joints into dish with devil mixture and spoon devil sauce all over them. Marinate for at least 1 hour, longer if possible, turning frequently.

3. Grill joints until brown all over, turning frequently. Grill 4 tomatoes at the same time. Serve with plain boiled rice and sauce made by adding ½ tin tomatoes and ¼ pint stock to remaining devil sauce. Heat sauce and strain. Serve with a green salad.

Smoked Turkey Salad

1 pound smoked turkey breast
½ pound noodles
2—3 tablespoons cream
2—3 lettuce hearts
3—4 tomatoes
3—4 oz cooked sweetcorn and green
   pepper

MAYONNAISE
½ teaspoon salt
¼ teaspoon pepper
½ level teaspoon dried mustard
½—¾ teaspoon sugar
1 egg (or 2 egg yolks)
¼—½ pint salad oil
1 tablespoon lemon juice
1—2 tablespoons wine vinegar

Thinly sliced smoked turkey on a layer of cooked noodles in mayonnaise, with tomatoes, lettuce and corn. This makes a filling first course, or part of an hors d'oeuvre (Serves 4—6, cold)

1. Make mayonnaise: Put pepper, mustard and sugar into liquidizer. Add egg. Mix thoroughly at low speed. Add a few drops of oil. Mix well. Then add remaining oil in steady stream until it has been absorbed and mayonnaise is very thick. Add lemon juice, vinegar, salt and 1—2 tablespoons boiling water, which thins it and helps to make it keep.

2. Boil noodles until tender in salted water, drain and let cool. Add beaten cream to mayonnaise, mix 2/3 with the cold noodles and season to taste.

3. Cut smoked turkey into very thin slices and place on top of noodle mayonnaise in a neat row. Garnish dish with lettuce hearts, peeled tomato quarters, and sweetcorn and green pepper mixed with a little of remaining mayonnaise.

Turkey Stuffed Tomatoes

4—6 oz cooked turkey chopped
4 large red tomatoes
½ cucumber
2 stalks celery
3—4 tablespoons cooked sweetcorn
¼ pint mayonnaise (approx.)
4 slices lemon or chopped parsley

A first course made with cold turkey, cucumber, celery and sweetcorn in mayonnaise, filled into large hollowed tomatoes and served with brown bread and butter (Serves 4, cold)

1. Chop cold turkey. Cut off the tops of the tomatoes, remove seeds, and reserve juice. Peel cucumber, dice, salt and leave for 20 minutes. Then wash and drain. Chop celery and mix with sweetcorn.

2. Make mayonnaise as in *Smoked Turkey Salad* (see above). Add juice from tomatoes.

3. Mix vegetables and turkey with enough mayonnaise to make creamy mixture. Fill into tomatoes, and garnish with sliced lemon or chopped parsley. Serve with brown bread and butter.

Turkey, Celery, Grape and Nut Salad

Chopped turkey, peeled grapes, sliced celery and almonds in orange flavoured mayonnaise, a delicious summer dish (Serves 4, cold)

8—10 oz turkey chopped
2—3 oz grapes
3—4 stalks celery
1½—2 oz almonds
juice of ½ lemon
grated rind of ½ orange
lettuce or endive leaves
¼ teaspoon paprika

1. Make mayonnaise as in *Smoked Turkey Salad* (see p. 9).

2. Chop turkey into medium size pieces. Peel grapes after dipping into boiling, then cold, water. Slice celery. Dip almonds in boiling water, remove skins, and brown halved nuts in moderate oven for 2 minutes.

3. Add extra lemon juice and grated orange rind to mayonnaise, to flavour. Mix turkey and other ingredients into mayonnaise. Arrange on lettuce or endive leaves and sprinkle with a little paprika.

Turkey with Lemon Mayonnaise

Sliced cooked turkey served with a refreshing lemon flavoured mayonnaise on a rice and vegetable salad (Serves 6—8, cold)

1½—2 pounds cooked turkey meat
1 pound rice
2—3 oz peas
2—3 oz green beans, chopped
2—3 oz sweetcorn
4 tomatoes
1 medium cucumber
1—1¼ pints mayonnaise (approx.)
grated rind of 2 lemons
1 tablespoon parsley chopped
6—8 thin slices lemon

FRENCH DRESSING
½ teaspoon French mustard
½—¾ pint oil
4—5 liquid oz wine vinegar
1—2 tablespoons fresh mixed herbs
   chopped

1. Boil rice in plenty of salt water for 10—12 minutes or according to instructions on package. Drain and wash well with cold water. Drain and dry. Boil peas, beans and sweetcorn in salt water. Drain and let cool. Peel and slice tomatoes, reserving juice. Peel cucumber, dice and sprinkle with salt. Leave for 20 minutes; then wash well and drain.

2. Make French dressing: Mix salt, pepper and sugar to taste with French mustard and oil. Add vinegar. Beat well. Add chopped herbs.

3. Make mayonnaise as in *Smoked Turkey Salad* (see p. 9) using double quantities and lemon instead of vinegar. Add 2—3 teaspoons grated lemon rind for flavour. Cut turkey into cubes or strips, mix with half the mayonnaise. Thin remaining mayonnaise slightly with the strained juice of the tomatoes.

4. Add all vegetables to cold cooked rice and moisten with French dressing. Arrange this mixture down sides of a dish. Spoon turkey mayonnaise down centre. Spoon little extra mayonnaise over the top. Sprinkle with chopped parsley mixed with remaining lemon rind, and garnish with slices of lemon made into twists.

Turkey Fricassee

Cold turkey re-heated in a cream sauce enriched with egg yolks and served with bacon rolls and fried mushrooms (Serves 4, hot)

1 pound cold turkey meat
3 oz butter (approx.)
1½ oz flour
½—¾ pint mixed stock and milk
½ teaspoon onion powder
1 tablespoon chopped parsley, thyme
   and powdered bay leaf
¼ teaspoon mace
2 egg yolks
3—4 tablespoons cream
4 rashers streaky bacon cut in half
8 mushrooms

Pre-heat oven to 325°F Mark 3
Pre-heat grill

1. Make white sauce: Melt 1½ oz butter, add flour, and pour on mixed chicken stock and milk. Blend well. Then bring to boil, stirring constantly. Simmer for few minutes. Then add onion powder, herbs and seasoning. Beat egg yolks with a little cream. Add a little sauce. Then strain egg yolk into sauce. Do not allow to boil.

2. Cut cold turkey into slices. Place in a buttered ovenproof dish. Cover with buttered paper. Heat in oven for 10—15 minutes. Spoon the sauce over turkey and return to oven for 10 minutes, being careful not to boil sauce.

3. Meanwhile, roll up bacon rashers and put on skewers. Grill until crisp. Put mushrooms into buttered dish with seasoning and a pat of butter on each. Cook in oven for 15 minutes at same time as turkey.

4. Arrange mushrooms around sides of dish and bacon rolls down centre and serve hot, with rice or mashed potatoes.

Turkey, Celery, Grape and Nut Salad (see p. 10)

Turkey Timbale

Finely minced cooked turkey mixed with white sauce and eggs, baked in a ring mould and filled with mushrooms cooked in a Madeira sauce (Serves 4, hot)

1. First make a thick cream sauce: Melt 1 oz butter, stir in 1 oz flour until blended. Pour in hot milk and bring to a boil stirring constantly. Cook for few minutes, add seasoning and allow to cool.

2. Mince turkey finely in liquidizer and mix with eggs beaten in cream. Add cooled sauce. Mix everything well together and turn into a thoroughly buttered ring mould allowing a little space at the top for expansion while cooking. Cover with a buttered paper. Put in roasting pan of hot water and bake for 25—35 minutes or until a skewer can be inserted into the centre and come out clean. Run a knife around the outside and inner ring of mould, and turn out on to a large round plate. Pour mushroom sauce into centre and serve at once.

3. While the timbale cooks, make mushroom sauce: Melt 1½ oz butter and cook quartered mushrooms for 2—3 minutes. Then sprinkle in 1 oz flour. Cook for 1 minute, remove from heat and add brown, well flavoured stock and blend thoroughly. Bring to a boil and simmer for a few minutes. Add seasoning, herbs and Worcestershire sauce and Madeira or sherry. Allow flavours to blend well before pouring into centre of mould.

8—12 oz turkey meat chopped
3 oz butter
2 oz flour
8 liquid oz milk flavoured with onion
 and herbs
2 eggs
3—4 tablespoons double cream
16—20 mushrooms
½—¾ pint well flavoured brown stock
1 tablespoon herbs chopped
2 teaspoons Worcestershire sauce
2—3 tablespoons Madeira or sherry

Pre-heat oven to 350°F Mark 4

Quickly made and tasty filling for French style pancakes, made with minced cold turkey and tinned condensed tomato soup or sauce, and finished with crispy cheesy topping (Serves 6, hot)

PANCAKES
8 oz flour
2 eggs
2 egg yolks
1 pint milk
½ oz butter
oil for frying

FILLING
10—12 oz turkey minced
1 tin condensed tomato soup (or equivalent sauce)
4—6 oz cooked vegetables (as available)
1—2 teaspoons tomato puree (if necessary)
¼ teaspoon onion powder
a pinch of garlic powder
1 oz butter
1 oz grated cheddar cheese

Pre-heat grill

Turkey and Tomato Pancakes

1. Sift flour with salt and pepper into bowl. Make a hollow in centre, and add beaten eggs and ¼ pint milk. Mix eggs and milk together with spoon before gradually drawing in flour. Add quarter pint of milk as mixture thickens. When it is smooth and like thick cream, beat for 5 minutes by hand or in mixer. Stir in melted butter and 6—8 liquid oz of milk. Leave batter in covered bowl for 30 minutes before cooking.

2. Test thickness of batter, which should just coat back of spoon. If too thick, add remaining milk and stir well. Grease a 5—6 inch griddle or frying pan with little oil. When hot, pour in enough batter to coat pan thinly. Cook until golden brown on one side, turn and cook other side. Pile up and keep warm. Allow 2—3 per person. (After frying, pancakes can be frozen. If using frozen pancakes, allow to defrost before filling.)

3. Mince turkey and mix with tin of condensed tomato soup. Add any cooked vegetables such as peas or sweetcorn, and herbs if available. Heat mixture and add a little tomato puree to taste, if desired. Sprinkle in a little onion and garlic powder, salt and pepper to taste.

4. Put filling into pancakes, roll up and place down centre of fireproof dish. Sprinkle with butter and cheese. Grill until cheese is golden brown and crisp. Serve at once.

Turkey and Mushroom Croquettes

Chopped cooked turkey and fresh mushrooms in a thick cream sauce enriched with egg yolk, shaped into small rolls, coated in egg and breadcrumbs, and fried in deep fat (Serves 4–6, hot)

8–10 oz cooked turkey chopped
2½–3 oz butter
2 oz flour for sauce
4 liquid oz strong turkey or chicken stock
4 liquid oz milk
salt, pepper
a pinch of mace
a small pinch of cayenne pepper
1 tablespoon parsley chopped
1½–2 oz mushrooms chopped
a little lemon juice
1 egg yolk
¼ pound seasoned flour
2 eggs beaten with 1 teaspoon oil
6 oz dried white breadcrumbs
fat for deep frying

1. Make thick sauce: Melt 2 oz butter and add flour. Add stock and milk, and bring to the boil. Cook until thick and smooth. Add seasonings and parsley and allow to cool.

2. Meanwhile, chop turkey into small pieces. Chop mushrooms and cook in ½ oz butter. Sprinkle with lemon juice. Add chopped turkey; then add sauce. Stir well. When almost cold add beaten egg yolk; put mixture into refrigerator to chill and set

3. Divide mixture into 12 equal portions. Shape each into small roll with floured fingers. Roll in seasoned flour, coating ends carefully. Brush all over with beaten egg and then cover thickly with dried white breadcrumbs.

4. Heat fat to 390°F or smoking hot. Fry 4 croquettes at a time until well browned. Then drain well and serve at once with a piquant brown or tomato sauce.

Turkey and Grape Aspic

Slices of cooked turkey and white grapes in layers of aspic, set in a round mould and turned out on watercress and lettuce (Serves 4–6, cold)

1. Make aspic: Melt gelatine in ½ pint clear hot turkey stock. When melted, add 4 tablespoons white wine, and 1 pint more of stock. Let cool thoroughly.

2. Meanwhile, dip white grapes into boiling water for 10 seconds, then into cold. Remove skins and pips and put in bowl with a little lemon juice to prevent browning. Cut turkey meat into neat small slices and cubes.

(cont.)

Turkey

(cont.)

1–1½ pounds turkey meat
¾–1 oz gelatine
1–1½ pints clear, well flavoured turkey
    stock
4 tablespoons white wine
1 pound white grapes (or ½ pound,
    and 1 tin of mandarin oranges)
juice of ½ lemon
a few tarragon leaves
lettuce and watercress

3. Pour a layer of aspic into a round mould. Arrange a decorative pattern of grapes with tarragon leaves and leave in refrigerator to set. Pour over another layer of aspic. Now put in a layer of turkey and repeat. Continue making layers of grapes, meat and aspic until all is used, allowing enough aspic to cover top completely.

4. Put in refrigerator and leave until set. Then dip in bowl of hot water to loosen jelly and turn out on to a salad-lined plate. This makes a good buffet dish or ladies' summer luncheon dish. Tinned mandarin oranges can be added or used in place of grapes.

Turkey Noodle Ring (See p. 15)

Turkey and Ham Patties

Crisp pastry patties with creamy filling of turkey and ham (Serves 4, hot)

4–5 oz turkey chopped
3–4 oz ham chopped
1 packet of frozen puff pastry, about
    1 pound
1 egg
1½ oz butter
1 onion
1¼ oz flour
½ pint milk
1 tablespoon parsley
salt, pepper, a pinch of mace

Pre-heat oven to 500°F Mark 10

1. Roll out pastry until ¼ inch thick. Using 2½ inch diameter pastry cutter, cut out 8 patties. Now using a smaller cutter, 1½ inch in diameter, make a central cut in each patty being careful not to cut through to the bottom. Brush surface of each patty with beaten egg. Do not allow egg to run over sides or this will prevent pastry rising.

2. Put on a dampened baking sheet and bake for about 15–20 minutes until patties have risen and are golden brown. Remove from oven, take off centre lids carefully and reserve. Scoop out the soft pastry inside and throw away. Keep warm.   *(cont.)*

(cont.)

3. Meanwhile make filling: Melt butter and cook finely chopped onion for 5—6 minutes to soften. Mix in flour. Add milk. Blend well before bringing to boil, stirring all the time. Add chopped turkey and ham, parsley and seasoning. Heat together and spoon into patty shells. Place lids on top and serve at once, or keep warm for a short time.

TURKEY: TASTY LEFTOVERS
Turkey Noodle Ring

A tasty way of using remains of cold turkey to make a filling family meal (Serves 4, hot)

8—10 oz cooked turkey
½ pound noodles
2½—3½ oz butter
3 onions
1 clove garlic
½ pint double cream (fresh or soured)
1 egg
2—3 tablespoons grated cheddar cheese
1 tablespoon herbs chopped
3 oz mushrooms
1 oz flour
¼ pint stock
¼ pint milk
4 oz cooked peas and sweetcorn
2 tablespoons cooked green pepper chopped
2 hard boiled eggs
a pinch of paprika

Pre-heat oven to 350°F Mark 4

1. Boil noodles in plenty of salted water until they are almost cooked. Drain. Heat 1½—2 oz butter in pan and cook 1 chopped onion and garlic for few minutes to soften. Stir noodles into this. Then add ½ pint cream (fresh or soured) beaten with egg, grated cheese and chopped herbs. Sprinkle liberally with salt and pepper, and mix thoroughly. Turn into a buttered ring mould and press in well. Cover with buttered paper and put in oven for 45 minutes to set and to finish cooking noodles. Remove when done, and turn out on a hot dish. Fill with turkey filling.

2. Melt 1—1½ oz butter and cook 2 finely sliced onions to soften for 5—6 minutes. Add mushrooms, stir well, then sprinkle in flour. Blend well. Add stock and milk. Bring to the boil and simmer for 4—5 minutes. Then remove from heat. Add chopped turkey meat, cooked peas, sweetcorn, green pepper and 2 hard boiled eggs quartered. Season well and allow to stand in a warm place until noodle ring is ready. Spoon into centre, and sprinkle with paprika.

Sliced Turkey in Chestnut Sauce

Delicious and unusual way of using cold sliced turkey in a chestnut flavoured sauce (Serves 4, hot)

8 large slices cooked turkey
1½ oz butter
2 onions
1 carrot
¾ oz flour
2 teaspoons tomato puree
1¼ pints brown stock
2 liquid oz sherry or wine (optional)
1 bay leaf
a few sprigs of parsley
1 sprig thyme
4—5 tablespoons chestnut puree or stuffing
3—4 roughly chopped cooked chestnuts
2 tomatoes (optional)

Pre-heat oven to 350°F Mark 4

1. Make sauce: Chop onions and carrots. Cook in melted butter until tender, about 10 minutes. Then brown gently. Add flour. When blended, add tomato puree and stock. A little sherry or wine can be added in place of some of the stock.) Bring to the boil, cook for 10—15 minutes adding herbs and seasoning. Strain through sieve, and add chestnut puree or stuffing. Re-heat and stir until smooth. Add a few pieces of cooked whole chestnuts to the sauce if available.

2. Cut turkey into thin slices and place in an ovenproof dish. Garnish with sliced tomatoes, if desired. Then spoon over sauce and reheat in oven for few minutes. Serve with crisp fried potatoes and green vegetables.

Turkey Cottage Pie

Chopped cooked turkey mixed with mushrooms, bacon and onions in white sauce, topped with a layer of creamy mashed potato and browned in oven (Serves 4, hot)

¾—1 pound chopped or diced cooked
   turkey
1 pound potatoes
3 onions
3 oz butter
¼ pint milk
2—3 rashers bacon
2 oz mushrooms chopped
1 tablespoon chopped parsley and
   tarragon
½ oz flour
a pinch of mace, salt, pepper
½—¾ pint turkey or chicken stock
2—3 tablespoons milk

Pre-heat oven to 400°F Mark 6

1. Peel potatoes and boil in salted water with 1 peeled onion to flavour. When tender, in 15—20 minutes, remove onion, drain potatoes. Mash thoroughly, beat in 1 oz butter and some warmed milk, enough to make a soft mixture without being at all runny. Heat carefully, adding salt, pepper and mace.

2. While potatoes boil, cook chopped onions gently to soften in 1—1½ oz butter. After 3 minutes add chopped bacon and after another 3 minutes add sliced mushrooms. Cook for 1 minute. Sprinkle in flour and when blended stir in stock, add herbs and seasoning. Bring mixture to the boil, simmer for a few minutes, and add diced or chopped turkey meat. Add a little milk. Then turn into an ovenproof dish.

3. Spread mashed potato carefully all over top of dish and smooth. Score potato with a fork and dot with tiny flakes of butter. Bake in oven for 20—30 minutes, or until surface of potato is golden brown and crisp.

Quick Turkey Hash

Chopped turkey heated gently with a tin of mushroom or asparagus soup, with added mushrooms and vegetables as available (Serves 4, hot)

10—15 oz cooked turkey meat chopped
1 tin condensed mushroom or
   asparagus soup
1 tin evaporated milk
3—4 sliced mushrooms if available
3—4 oz cooked peas, beans, sweetcorn,
   tomato etc.
1 tablespoon chopped herbs or 2—3
   tablespoons grated cheese

1. Empty tin of condensed soup into pan and heat with enough added milk to make consistency of sauce. Add sliced mushrooms if available and cook gently for 4—5 minutes. Then add chopped turkey meat and any available cooked vegetables.

2. Heat the hash gently until completely hot; then add herbs or grated cheese. Serve hot with rice or mashed potatoes.

Fried Turkey Crisps

Chopped turkey in sauce with bacon, mushroom and cheese, made into round balls, coated in egg and breadcrumbs, and fried in deep fat until crisp (Serves 4-6, hot)

4—6 oz cold turkey chopped
1½ oz butter
1 tablespoon chopped onion
4 rashers bacon
2 oz chopped mushrooms
1½ oz flour
8 liquid oz stock
3 egg yolks
2 tablespoons grated Italian cheese
2 tablespoons breadcrumbs
2—4 oz flour seasoned with salt, pepper
   and paprika
2 eggs
4—6 oz dry white breadcrumbs

1. Melt butter, cook chopped onion and diced streaky bacon for 3—4 minutes. Then add finely chopped mushrooms, cook again for 2 minutes, sprinkle in flour and blend smoothly. Add stock and when thoroughly mixed bring mixture to a boil, stirring constantly. Cook for 2 minutes and let cool slightly. Add beaten egg yolks and seasoning, cheese and breadcrumbs. Allow to cool completely in refrigerator.

2. Form tablespoonsful of the mixture into balls. Roll in seasoned flour. Brush thoroughly with beaten egg all over. Then shake in a bag of dry white breadcrumbs until completely coated.

3. Heat fat to 360°F (until a cube of bread turns brown in 1 minute). Cook crisps until brown all over, remove and drain on paper towel. Serve at once, very hot, with a sharp tomato sauce.

Turkey Salad in Curried Mayonnaise

Shreds of turkey on a salad of cold cooked vegetables coated with curry flavoured mayonnaise, suitable as a first course or part of hors d'oeuvre or summer salad (Serves 4–6, cold)

¾–1 pound turkey meat
12–15 oz mixed cooked vegetables, peas, beans, sweetcorn, celery and green pepper
4 tomatoes
1 bunch watercress
½ oz butter
1 shallot (or 1 tablespoon chopped onion)
2 teaspoons curry powder
1 teaspoon flour
¼ pint stock
2 teaspoons coconut
2 teaspoons chutney
3 teaspoons lemon juice
½–¾ pint mayonnaise
a pinch of paprika
1–2 lemons

1. Cook vegetables separately, and allow to cool. Shred cold turkey. Quarter tomatoes, remove seeds, strain and reserve juice for thinning mayonnaise. Wash watercress and dry thoroughly.

2. Make curry flavouring: Melt butter, cook chopped shallot or onion until tender. Add curry powder or paste and cook for a minute or two. Sprinkle in flour and cook for 1 minute. Add stock and blend well. Then bring to boil, stirring all the time. Sprinkle on coconut, add chutney and lemon juice, and cook for 10–15 minutes. Then strain and allow to cool. Add lemon juice, salt and pepper. When cold, add to mayonnaise.

3. Make mayonnaise as in *Smoked Turkey Salad* (see p. 9). Add cooled curry mixture to taste. Add as much of strained tomato juice as will make spooning consistency.

4. Mix all vegetables together and season with salt and pepper, sprinkle with lemon juice. Put into dish or salad bowl. Arrange turkey shreds in centre, spoon mayonnaise carefully over the top allowing the vegetable salad to show around edges. Sprinkle top with paprika. Arrange tomato quarters and small sprigs of watercress alternately around the edge of dish and serve with lemon quarters separately.

Smothered Turkey

Slices of cooked turkey on a bed of cooked rice, covered with a soured cream sauce and topped with chopped chives (Serves 4, hot)

8 large slices of cold turkey
¾ pound rice
1½ oz butter
1 onion
½ pint soured cream
a pinch of nutmeg
2 tablespoons chives chopped

Pre-heat oven to 350°F Mark 4

1. Cook rice in boiling salt water. Drain and rinse with hot water. Dry and put in the bottom of a serving dish.

2. Cut cold turkey into slices and place over rice. Cover with buttered paper and heat through in oven for 15–20 minutes.

3. Melt butter and cook finely chopped onion until tender but not brown, 6–8 minutes. Add soured cream. Blend well. Add salt, pepper and a little nutmeg.

4. Spoon soured cream sauce over turkey and rice and sprinkle with chopped chives. Serve at once.

Turkey Gratin

¾–1 pound chopped cooked turkey (or other poultry or game)
1½ oz butter
1 onion
2–3 large mushrooms
1¼ oz flour
½–¾ pint stock
3–6 oz cooked vegetables, (peas, beans, sweetcorn, chopped carrots, green pepper, etc, or 1 cup cooked noodles)
3–4 tablespoons double cream
1 tablespoon chopped parsley and thyme
3–4 tablespoons grated cheddar cheese

Pre-heat grill

Useful way of using leftover turkey and cooked vegetables, in a tasty sauce topped with browned grated cheese (Serves 4–6, hot)

1. Melt butter and cook chopped onion until tender. Add chopped mushrooms and cook for 1 minute. Sprinkle in flour and blend well. Pour on stock and bring to boil, stirring constantly. Add chopped turkey and any available cooked vegetables or cooked noodles. Stir well into sauce. Add herbs and cream.

2. Turn into buttered baking dish and sprinkle thickly with grated cheese and a little paprika. Grill until crisp and brown all over. Serve with cooked noodles, rice or potatoes.

CHICKEN: PARTY DISHES

Chicken Maryland

6 pieces frying chicken
4 tablespoons flour mixed with salt, pepper and a pinch of cayenne pepper
1 egg
1 teaspoon oil
4—5 oz fresh white breadcrumbs
2 tablespoons oil
3—3½ oz butter
3 bananas
6 rashers bacon

FRITTERS
3—4 oz sweetcorn
1 egg
4 oz self raising flour
¼—½ teaspoon curry powder
fat for deep frying

SAUCE
1½ oz butter
1 onion
1 clove garlic
1 small tin tomatoes
1 level tablespoon mixed herbs
½ teaspoon sugar
½ teaspoon paprika
¼ pint cider or stock

Pre-heat grill

Particularly delicious dish of fried chicken served with fried bananas, sweetcorn fritters, bacon rolls, and a savoury tomato sauce (Serves 6, hot)

1. Roll chicken pieces in seasoned flour, then brush all over with egg beaten with oil and coat well with fresh white breadcrumbs. Heat oil and add 2—2½ oz butter. When foaming, put in chicken pieces and fry gently for 20—25 minutes, turning frequently until brown and crisp all over.

2. Meanwhile, prepare sweetcorn fritters: Drain tinned sweetcorn and mix with 1 egg yolk and seasoning. Sift flour and curry powder, stir into sweetcorn mixture. Just before frying, beat egg white and fold into sweetcorn mixture. Heat fat until very hot but not smoking, 370°F. Drop fritter mixture into fat by tablespoonsful and fry until light brown. Drain on paper towel. Keep warm.

3. Fry halved bananas in 1 oz butter until golden brown. Keep warm. Cut bacon rashers in half, roll up carefully. Thread on to skewers, grill until crisp all over. Keep warm.

4. Prepare tomato sauce: Melt butter, cook sliced onion and crushed garlic for 5—6 minutes. Add tomatoes, herbs, seasoning, sugar, paprika and cider or stock. Bring to the boil, then strain or blend in liquidizer and serve hot with chicken.

Chicken Burgundy

1 capon or chicken 3—4 pounds
4 rashers unsmoked bacon
12—16 small onions
12—16 button mushrooms
1 clove garlic
2 oz butter
½ pint burgundy or red wine
½—¾ pint strong brown stock
2—3 sprigs parsley or 1 teaspoon dried parsley
1 sprig thyme or a pinch of dried thyme
1 bay leaf

Pre-heat oven to 325°F Mark 3

Rich burgundy flavoured casserole of chicken, bacon, onions and mushrooms (Serves 4—6, hot)

1. Thaw the capon or chicken if frozen. Cut it into suitably sized pieces and dry. Chop bacon into small pieces. Peel onions and mushrooms. Crush garlic.

2. Melt 1—1½ oz butter and fry bacon, onions and garlic until golden brown. Remove to casserole and keep warm. Fry chicken pieces in same butter until golden brown all over. Remove to casserole.

3. Pour the red wine into pan and bring to a boil to reduce quantity to half. Meanwhile, flambé wine to burn off the alcohol. Add the stock and boil for 5 minutes. Season with salt and black pepper. Pour this sauce over chicken and vegetables in casserole. Add herbs. Bring to the boil. Then reduce heat and cook for 45—60 minutes over low heat or in oven.

4. While chicken is cooking melt remaining butter and cook the mushrooms. Add to casserole for last 20 minutes of cooking time.

French Roast Chicken

Chicken roasted with butter, herbs and well flavoured stock. Best method of cooking chicken to be eaten cold (Serves 4–6, hot or cold)

1. If frozen, be sure chicken is completely thawed out before cooking. Make stock with giblets, onion, seasoning and water. Cook slowly for 15 minutes. Put ½ the butter inside bird with herbs, salt and pepper. Spread remaining butter over chicken, cover with fat bacon, put into roasting pan and pour half the stock over the chicken.

2. Cook in oven, basting with stock every 15 minutes and turning the bird from side to side. Allow 20 minutes per pound weight. For last 20 minutes remove bacon and place bird breast up to brown.

3. Remove bird on to hot dish and keep hot in oven. Meanwhile skim the butter from top of pan drippings. Add remaining stock to roasting pan and boil until well flavoured. Serve as gravy.

4. Serve chicken either hot or cold with a green salad and garnished with watercress.

1 chicken, 3—4 pounds
chicken giblets and 1 onion (or 1 chicken cube)
½—¾ pint water
3—3½ oz butter
3—4 sprigs of fresh parsley
2—3 slices fat bacon
1 bunch watercress

Pre-heat oven to 375°F Mark 6

Circassian Chicken

Unusual Middle Eastern dish of chicken in walnut sauce, flavoured with paprika and cayenne
(Serves 4–6, hot)

1. Put chicken in deep pan and just cover with cold water. Add 3 onions each stuck with a clove, chopped celery, herbs, peppercorns and a little salt. Bring to the boil and simmer until tender, about 1 hour. Skim as necessary. Drain and keep warm, reserving stock for sauce.

2. Grind walnuts finely in liquidizer and mix with breadcrumbs. Melt butter and cook 2 chopped onions and crushed garlic until golden brown and soft. Then add to walnut mixture, blending carefully. When quite smooth, cook until it reaches boiling point, adding more stock if sauce becomes too thick. Season with salt and a little pepper.

3. Mix oil, paprika and cayenne pepper together, and when oil is red, strain. Add enough of this oil to walnut sauce to make it a delicate pink.

4. Cut chicken into pieces. Put a layer of sauce in the bottom of a fireproof dish, lay chicken pieces on top. Spoon remaining sauce over the top of the chicken. Reheat thoroughly. Decorate top with remaining red oil, sprinkling over surface of dish. Serve with plain boiled rice.

1 chicken, 3–4 pounds
5 onions
3 cloves
3 stalks celery
a few sprigs parsley
1 bay leaf
8 peppercorns
8 oz shelled walnuts
2 oz dry breadcrumbs
1 oz butter
1 clove garlic
2 teaspoons paprika
a pinch of cayenne pepper
3 tablespoons oil

Chicken Curry

4 large chicken pieces
2½ oz butter
2 medium onions
1 tablespoon curry powder (or more according to taste)
1 teaspoon curry paste
½ oz flour
1½ cups strong chicken stock
1 apple
1 oz raisins
2 tablespoons chutney
1 bay leaf
2 tablespoons finely shredded coconut
juice of ½ lemon
2 teaspoons redcurrant or other sharp jelly
¾—1¼ pounds cooked long grain rice
2—3 teaspoons turmeric powder
1 lemon
½ teaspoon paprika

Pre-heat oven to 350°F Mark 4

Tender chicken pieces browned in butter and cooked in a mild curry sauce, served with plain boiled rice and numerous accompaniments (Serves 4, hot)

1. Heat butter, and brown chicken pieces until golden. Remove and put in a fireproof dish to keep warm.

2. Slice onions finely and cook until golden brown. Then add curry powder and paste, and cook for few minutes. Add flour and allow to brown slightly. Add stock, bring to boil and simmer for 4—5 minutes. Then add chopped apple, raisins, chutney, bay leaf and salt. Cook together for 1 minute. Pour over chicken pieces, and cook in oven for 35—40 minutes, by which time chicken pieces should be nearly tender.

3. Meanwhile, pour 2—3 liquid oz of boiling water over shredded coconut; let stand for 30 minutes. Strain liquid on to chicken, adding lemon juice and jelly. Cook for 15 minutes.

4. When cooked, remove chicken pieces and put in centre of a ring of boiled rice finished with turmeric cooked in remaining butter. Boil up sauce, sieve or liquidize it, season to taste, and spoon over chicken. Garnish with thin slices of lemon and sprinkle with paprika.

Brunswick Stew (see p. 32)

Chicken Suprême with Mushrooms

Tender breasts of chicken cooked in butter, served on sliced cooked mushrooms and covered with a delicately flavoured cream sauce (Serves 4, hot)

4 chicken breasts
3½—4 oz butter
10—12 large mushrooms
2 teaspoons lemon juice
1 tablespoon parsley chopped
1½ oz flour
½ pint chicken stock
salt, white pepper
a large pinch of mace
¼ pint cream
2 egg yolks
1—2 tablespoons white wine (or a little lemon juice)

Pre-heat oven to 375°F Mark 5

1. Remove 4 complete chicken breasts or "supremes" from 2 chickens, (use remaining chicken parts for another meal). Melt 2—2½ oz butter in a pan large enough to hold all 4 chicken breasts. Cook them in butter very gently, without browning, for 4—5 minutes on each side. Remove from pan and put into a buttered dish, cover with foil and bake in oven for about 10—15 minutes, or until tender and cooked through.

2. Meanwhile, cook sliced mushrooms in butter left from chicken and 1 teaspoon lemon juice for 5—6 minutes. Season; add chopped parsley. Place in bottom of serving dish and when chicken is cooked place "supremes" on top. Reduce oven to 250°F Mark ¾ and keep warm while making sauce.

3. Melt 1½ oz butter and stir in flour. When smooth, add stock and bring slowly to the boil, stirring constantly. Cook for 2 minutes. Add salt, white pepper and mace. Mix cream with egg yolks. Mix 3—4 tablespoons hot sauce with cream and eggs; strain carefully into sauce, stirring constantly. Re-heat very gently over a pan of hot water. Do not allow sauce to reach boiling point or eggs will curdle and sauce be ruined. Season to taste and add a little white wine or lemon juice, if desired. Spoon over chicken "supremes" and serve with boiled rice.

Chicken Veronique

Tender chicken roasted in the French manner, served with a white wine sauce and garnished with peeled white grapes (Serves 4, hot)

1 roasting chicken, about 3 pounds
3–3½ oz butter
few sprigs tarragon (or dried tarragon)
1¼ pints stock made with chicken
    giblets (or chicken bouillon cube
    and water)
2 slices fat bacon
4–6 oz white grapes
little lemon juice
¾–1¼ pounds plain boiled rice

SAUCE
1½ oz flour
¾ pint strong chicken stock
¼ pint white wine
2–3 tablespoons heavy cream

Pre-heat oven to 375°F Mark 5

1. Roast chicken as in *French Roast Chicken* (see p. 19) using tarragon as flavouring inside the bird.

2. Meanwhile, dip grapes in boiling water for 10 seconds and then in cold. Peel (and remove pips if necessary). Put grapes in small bowl and sprinkle with lemon juice to prevent browning.

3. Remove chicken from roasting pan when cooked, and carve. Place pieces on rice, cover and keep warm.

4. Skim off 3 oz butter into a saucepan. Heat gently, sprinkle in flour, blend carefully, pour on stock and wine and bring to the boil, stirring constantly. Boil for few minutes, remove from heat and allow to cool slightly. Add cream and grapes. Allow grapes to warm through. Then spoon sauce over chicken, and serve at once.

Chicken à la King

An especially delicious way of using cold chicken to make a party filling for pastry cases, or served on fried croutons, with mushrooms and sweet pimentos in a creamy sauce (Serves 4, hot)

8–10 oz cooked chicken
1 sweet red or green pepper
8 mushrooms
1½ oz butter
a squeeze of lemon juice
1 oz flour
½ pint stock
2 tablespoons sherry
a pinch of mace
2 egg yolks
3–4 tablespoons double cream
4 pastry patty shells or 4 fried rounds
    of bread
1 teaspoon chopped parsley or ¼
    teaspoon paprika

1. Chop the pepper and boil for 5 minutes. Rinse in cold water; drain. Cook sliced mushrooms in ½ oz butter and a little lemon juice until tender, 5–6 minutes. Dice cooked chicken into small pieces.

2. Make sauce: Melt butter and blend in flour smoothly. Add chicken stock, bring to the boil, stirring constantly, simmer for few minutes, then add sherry, mace and seasoning.

3. Mix chicken, mushrooms and peppers into sauce, put in top of double boiler. Mix egg yolks and cream together. Add a little of the hot sauce, stir, strain and add to chicken. Heat carefully; do not boil.

4. Spoon mixture into hot pastry patty shells or on to fried rounds of bread. Sprinkle the top with chopped parsley or paprika, serve at once.

Paella

A delicious Spanish dish of chicken, prawns, clams or mussels, in saffron, onion and garlic flavoured rice (Serves 4–6, hot)

4–6 large chicken pieces seasoned
    with salt and pepper
4–5 tablespoons olive or corn oil
2 onions
1–2 cloves garlic
¾–1 pound long grain rice
1¼–1½ pints chicken stock (or chicken
    bouillon cube and water)
large pinch of saffron
1–1½ oz butter
3 tomatoes
pinch of mace
1–2 tablespoons chopped parsley and
    thyme
2 oz peas (or green beans)
4–6 oz unshelled prawns or 12 mussels
    or 4–6 clams

Pre-heat oven to 350°F Mark 4

1. Heat oil in a large flat frying pan and when hot cook chicken pieces for 12–15 minutes until golden brown all over. Remove and keep warm.

2. Add sliced onions and crushed garlic to pan, and cook for 5–6 minutes, until golden brown. Add rice and fry for 1 minute, stirring constantly to prevent sticking.

3. Add stock, saffron soaked in 2 tablespoons of hot stock, butter, and peeled and chopped tomatoes. Bring to the boil; then add chicken pieces. Add seasoning, herbs, peas (or beans) and simmer for 10 minutes.

4. Add prawns, mussels or clams to pan and heat in oven for 15 minutes; by this time the shells of the mussels and clams should have opened. Serve very hot.

Barbecued Chicken

4 large chicken quarters or halves
BARBECUE SAUCE
4—5 tablespoons oil
1 onion
1 clove garlic
1 medium tin tomatoes (or 3—4
   tablespoons tomato puree)
1 tablespoon tomato ketchup
1 tablespoon chutney
1 tablespoon vinegar
¼ pint stock (or water)
1 tablespoon Worcestershire sauce
1 teaspoon French mustard
1 teaspoon paprika
juice and grated rind of ½ lemon
2 level teaspoons brown sugar
1 tablespoon parsley finely chopped
1 teaspoon mixed powdered thyme,
   nutmeg and bay leaf

Tender chicken pieces grilled in a spicy sauce over a charcoal grill (Serves 4, hot)

1. Prepare barbecue sauce: Heat oil and cook finely chopped onion and crushed garlic for 5 minutes, add sieved tomatoes or puree and all other ingredients. Cook for 20—30 minutes, season to taste, strain and allow to cool.

2. With a sharp knife make small cuts into the chicken pieces. Spoon the cold barbecue sauce over them and let stand for at least ½ hour.

3. Heat charcoal, electric or gas grill. Place chicken pieces on hot grill and turn every 5—6 minutes, basting frequently with barbecue sauce. Allow 30—45 minutes to barbecue quarters depending on heat of grill and thickness of chicken pieces. Test with skewer: if juice from chicken runs clear the chicken is cooked through.

4. Heat remaining sauce, and serve chicken with salad and baked potatoes.

Chicken Cordon Bleu

Chicken breasts stuffed with a mixture of chopped ham and Swiss cheese with garlic, coated in egg and breadcrumbs, and fried in butter (Serves 4, hot)

4 chicken breasts
4 level tablespoons chopped cooked ham
4 level tablespoons grated Swiss cheese
1 small clove garlic
1—2 tablespoons white wine
3—4 tablespoons seasoned flour
1 large egg
2 liquid oz oil
2—3 oz dried white breadcrumbs
2—2½ oz butter

1. Place 4 chicken breasts skin side downwards, and with a sharp knife cut a shallow slit down centre of each without cutting through to skin. Then cut shallow pockets on either side of these slits.

2. Mix ham and cheese with crushed garlic and a little white wine to moisten. Season well. Fill into pockets in chicken breasts and seal slit with the small finger-shaped fillet which is attached to each breast. Put in fridge to chill for thirty minutes.

3. Coat well in seasoned flour, brush carefully with egg beaten with 1 teaspoon of oil, and roll in breadcrumbs. Heat oil, and add butter. When foaming, fry chicken breasts until tender, golden brown and crisp all over. Drain on paper towel.

4. Serve with asparagus spears or broccoli, and a party salad.

Paprika Chicken

A spicy paprika flavoured chicken dish, garnished with soured cream (Serves 4, hot)

1 chicken 2½—3 pounds
2 tablespoons flour seasoned with salt
   and pepper
2 tablespoons oil
2 oz butter
4 onions
1 clove garlic
2 teaspoons paprika
2 tablespoons tomato puree
½ pint white wine
½ pint strong chicken stock
1 tablespoon chopped parsley
1 teaspoon thyme
1 carton or 5 liquid oz soured cream

1. Cut chicken into pieces and roll in seasoned flour. Heat oil. Add 1 oz butter. When foaming, add chicken pieces and fry until golden brown. Remove and put into casserole.

2. Add remaining butter and sliced onions to frying pan. Cover and cook until tender but not brown, about 5—6 minutes. Add crushed garlic; cook for 1 minute. Add paprika and remaining seasoned flour, then the tomato puree. Stir until smooth. Then add wine and stock. Bring to the boil, stirring constantly.

3. Pour sauce over chicken pieces. Add herbs, salt and pepper to taste. Cook slowly until tender, for about 1 hour.

4. Spoon soured cream over top of casserole, and serve with buttered noodles or rice.

Chicken Kiev

A luxurious dish of fried chicken breasts, stuffed with garlic and herb flavoured butter (Serves 4, hot)

1. Mix butter with finely crushed garlic, chopped herbs, lemon juice and seasoning, shape into a roll about 3—4 inches long. Wrap in foil and put into refrigerator to freeze.

2. Each chicken breast consists of one large heart shaped piece and a long thin finger shaped piece. The smaller pieces flatten out slightly. Place the large pieces skin side down and make a shallow slit down centre of each. Then make a shallow pocket to each side with a sharp knife. Remove skin. Cut butter roll into 4 long pieces, place one piece on each chicken breast so that it is in the pocket. Place flattened smaller pieces of chicken over butter and then close the slits over them. Turn ends of chicken and shape each breast neatly. Wrap each in foil and put into the refrigerator for at least 30 minutes to firm.

3. Just before cooking, roll each breast in seasoned flour, then brush with egg beaten with oil and cover thickly with dried white breadcrumbs.

4. Heat fat (or oil) until a cube of fresh bread takes 60 seconds to brown. Fry chicken breasts for 5—7 minutes, until golden brown and crisp. Serve at once with boiled rice and lemon quarters. (Warn guests to cut chicken carefully or hot butter will spurt out.)

4 whole breasts of chicken
3 oz butter
1 clove garlic
1 tablespoon mixed parsley, tarragon
 and lemon thyme
1 tablespoon lemon juice
2 oz flour
2 eggs
1 teaspoon oil
4—6 oz dried white breadcrumbs
fat (or oil) for deep frying
1 lemon

Chicken in Lemon Sauce

Lemon flavoured chicken casserole garnished with mushrooms and parsley (Serves 4, hot)

1. Lightly brown seasoned chicken pieces in 2 oz butter in fireproof dish or casserole. Remove and keep warm.

2. Chop onions, quarter carrots, slice celery and cook for 5—10 minutes in the butter to soften, without browning. Put chicken pieces back into casserole on top of vegetables, sprinkle with grated rind of ½ lemon and all the juice; pour in stock and wine. Add parsley sprigs, bay leaf and lemon thyme if available. Season and cook in oven for 35—40 minutes, or until chicken pieces are tender.

3. Remove chicken to a serving dish and keep warm. Remove carrots, the bay leaf and herb stalks. Then sieve or liquidize remaining vegetables. Reheat the lemon and vegetable sauce, and if too thick add enough chicken stock to thin. Check for lemon flavour and add more lemon juice if necessary, to taste.

4. Melt remaining butter and cook the baby mushrooms for 3—4 minutes until tender and place on top of chicken. Spoon sauce over chicken and mushrooms. Cut remaining lemon rind into match-like strips, boil for 2 minutes, drain and dip in cold water to revive colour. Sprinkle over dish with finely chopped parsley.

4 chicken quarters seasoned with salt
 and pepper
3 oz butter
2 small onions or shallots
2 carrots
2 stalks celery
1 large lemon
½—¾ pint chicken stock
¼ pint white wine
3—4 parsley sprigs
1 bay leaf
a sprig of lemon thyme
4 oz baby mushrooms
1 tablespoon parsley finely chopped

Pre-heat oven to 350°F Mark 4

Traditional Roast Chicken

Chicken stuffed and roasted, served with crisp bacon rolls, grilled chippolata sausages and bread sauce (Serves 4—6, hot)

1 chicken or capon, 3—4 pounds (if frozen thaw completely)
6 oz of butter
1 large onion
4—6 oz fresh breadcrumbs
2 tablespoons chopped cooked ham
1 tablespoon chopped parsley
½ teaspoon chopped thyme
a little grated lemon rind
1 beaten egg or 2—3 tablespoons milk
2—3 tablespoons bacon fat or oil
¾ pint chicken stock made from giblets (or a chicken bouillon cube)
4—6 rashers bacon
8—12 chippolata sausages
BREAD SAUCE
½ pint milk
1 onion
2—3 cloves
½ bay leaf
3 parsley sprigs or 1 teaspoon dried parsley
a pinch of mace or nutmeg
6 peppercorns
2—2½ oz fresh breadcrumbs
½ oz butter
2 tablespoons cream

Pre-heat oven to 400°F Mark 6

1. First prepare stuffing: Melt 2—3 oz butter, cook ½ onion, chopped, for 3—4 minutes to soften. Mix with breadcrumbs, chopped ham, herbs and grated lemon rind. Add seasoning, beaten egg or milk to make fairly moist mixture. Fill into neck end of chicken. Fold skin flap under wings and skewer or sew to hold in place. Put ½ onion and some seasoning inside cavity of bird with a little butter. Rub remaining butter over chicken and sprinkle with seasoning.

2. Melt bacon fat or oil in roasting pan. When hot, add chicken, baste thoroughly, then cover with foil and put into oven. Roast, basting every 15 minutes, turning chicken from side to side, allowing 20 minutes per pound and a little extra time. During the last 15 minutes, remove foil to allow breast to brown. Remove to hot dish and keep warm while making gravy. Pour off fat, pour in remaining chicken stock, bring to the boil. To obtain flavour, reduce liquid by boiling.

3. Meanwhile, prepare bread sauce. Stick cloves into onion, put in pan with milk, herbs, peppercorns. Cook gently for 20—30 minutes without boiling. Strain on to fresh breadcrumbs; heat together until creamy, then at the last minute stir in butter and cream. Add seasoning and serve hot.

4. Divide bacon rashers in half, make into rolls; put on skewers and grill until crisp at the same time as grilling chippolata sausages. Serve chicken surrounded by bacon rolls and sausages, the gravy and bread sauce separately.

Chicken Stuffed with Mushrooms

Spring chickens stuffed with mushrooms, roasted and finished with a cream sauce (Serves 4, hot)

2 small spring chickens or petits poussins
3—4 oz mushrooms
4 oz butter
1 small onion
2—3 liquid oz single cream
1 level teaspoon cornflour (optional)
a little chopped parsley or paprika

Pre-heat oven to 350°F Mark 4

1. Cook finely chopped onion for about 5 minutes in half the butter with lid on pan. Slice or quarter mushrooms, add to onions and cook for 3—4 minutes. Season and allow to cool.

2. Wipe the prepared spring chickens; stuff them with the cooled mushroom mixture. Melt remaining butter in fireproof dish or iron casserole. Fry chickens gently until brown all over. Season and pour over 2 liquid oz water. Cook in oven for about 20 minutes. When tender remove from casserole and split each bird in half. Arrange on warm serving dish and put into low oven while making sauce.

3. Make sauce: Mix cream with gravy in casserole, bring slowly to a boil and season to taste. The sauce will be fairly thin: to thicken, if preferred, mix cornflour with 2—3 tablespoons of cold water until smooth. Add to hot sauce and boil for ½ minute.

4. Spoon a little of this sauce over each bird and serve the rest separately. Decorate with a little chopped parsley or a sprinkling of paprika.

Chicken and Cheesy Rice Ring (see p. 35)

CHICKEN: COLD BUFFETS
Chicken Liver Paté

A rich smooth liver paté decorated with chilled consomme and mushrooms, suitable as first course or cold buffet (Serves 8–10, cold)

1 pound chicken livers (fresh or frozen)
8 oz butter
2 onions
1 large clove garlic (optional)
1 small glass sherry or brandy
1 tablespoonful fresh mixed herbs:
  parsley, lemon thyme, basil,
  marjoram, and summer savory (or
  2 level teaspoons dried herbs)
a pinch of dried mace (optional)
GARNISH
1 tin consomme
3–4 oz button mushrooms
1 bunch watercress

1. Fry finely chopped onions and crushed garlic gently in 3 oz butter for a few minutes. Do not allow to brown as this will ruin the flavour. Add chicken livers and cook for 3–4 minutes. Then add mixed herbs, mace and seasoning. Cook for 1 minute. Remove from stove and let cool.

2. Mash livers to a soft pulp in liquidizer, stirring in 3–4 oz melted butter. Add sherry or brandy. Put the paté into a serving dish, or a lightly oiled mould so that it can be turned out after chilling. It can be made several days before a party if kept in the refrigerator and should be a delicate pink inside when cut.

3. Make garnish: Chop chilled consomme and place around paté. Cook mushrooms gently for a few minutes in remaining melted butter until completely absorbed. Drain on paper towel. Let cool. Decorate the top of the paté with mushrooms and surround with watercress.

Chicken Jelly

Pretty and delicious jellied chicken and vegetable dish suitable for summer buffet party or luncheon (Serves 4–6, cold)

8–12 oz cold chicken meat
2 tins consomme
½–¾ oz gelatine
2 tablespoons sherry
2 eggs
3 tomatoes
4–5 oz mixed peas, carrots, sweetcorn
1 lettuce
1 bunch watercress

1. Dissolve gelatine in the hot consomme, add sherry and allow to cool. Hard boil eggs for 10–12 minutes and put into cold water to cool thoroughly. Cut up cold chicken meat into long strips, peel and quarter tomatoes. Set aside. Cook vegetables until tender, drain and cook.

2. Pour a layer of consomme into a mould; put in refrigerator to set. Cut hard-boiled eggs into slices and arrange a layer on the chilled consomme in mould with tomato quarters in between. Spoon some more consomme over them and again allow to set. Arrange chicken and vegetables and remaining egg in layers with the consomme, letting each layer set.

3. Chill thoroughly in refrigerator and when set, dip outside of mould for a few seconds into hot water to loosen. Turn out on to serving dish. Garnish with lettuce and watercress.

Chicken Tetrazzini (see p. 33)

Chicken Galantine

Boned chicken stuffed with sausage meat and tongue forcemeat, boiled until tender; when cold coated with a chaudfroid white sauce and set with jelly coating, a buffet or party dish (Serves 6–8, cold)

1. If possible, buy chicken ready boned, otherwise remove bones with a very sharp knife, first cutting down back and loosening skin and flesh from carcass without piercing skin. Remove bones from legs and wings in same manner. Then place bird skin side downwards and season.

2. Put carcass and giblets into large pan with onions, carrots, celery, peppercorns and herbs. Cover with water, cook for as long as possible to make a well flavoured stock. *(cont.)*

1 stewing or roasting chicken, 3½—4
   pounds
2 onions
2 carrots
2 stalks celery
8 peppercorns
parsley, thyme and a bay leaf
8—12 oz sausage meat
½ level teaspoon onion powder
2 tablespoons parsley chopped
½ teaspoon chopped thyme
1 teaspoon grated lemon rind and little
   juice
2 hard boiled eggs
2 oz chopped tongue
3—4 closed button mushrooms
a squeeze of lemon juice

CHAUDFROID SAUCE
1½ oz butter
1½ oz flour
¾ pint milk, flavoured with onion and
   herbs
½ oz gelatine
3—4 tablespoons double cream

ASPIC JELLY
½ oz gelatine
¾ pint strong chicken stock
2 tablespoons sherry

3. Mix sausage meat with seasoning, onion powder, chopped parsley, thyme, lemon rind and juice. Place half this mixture down centre of chicken and a layer of sliced hard boiled egg and chopped tongue on top. Place half remaining sausage meat on top, using other half to stuff legs and wings.

4. Re-shape bird as well as possible, tidily folding in loose ends of skin at neck and opening. Allow the skin which was cut down back to overlap slightly. Sew up tightly with clean white string. Wrap chicken in clean cloth or muslin, put in suitably sized pan, cover with stock and cook very gently for 2—3 hours according to size and age of bird. Check from time to time to make sure that there is enough liquid to cover bird which should be turned once after 1—1½ hours.

Chicken Chop Suey (see p. 33)

5. When cooked, remove from pot and when slightly cool improve shape if necessary. Allow to get cold, preferably overnight. Remove string.

6. Make white or cream sauce with butter, flour and milk, add gelatine dissolved in hot stock and when cool add cream. When it begins to set and has consistency of thick cream, put chicken on cake rack and spoon mixture over entire surface. Allow to set. Cook sliced mushrooms in a little stock and lemon juice until tender. Cool, then place carefully down centre of bird to decorate.

7. Dissolve gelatine in hot stock with sherry and let it cool. When it begins to set spoon carefully all over the chaudfroid sauce on chicken. Let it cool completely in refrigerator, and serve on dish decorated with lettuce, sliced cucumber, tomatoes and radish flowers.

Dessert apples stuffed with diced chicken and fruit in mayonnaise, suitable for buffet party or summer lunch (Serves 4, cold)

8 oz white cooked chicken meat
½ pint mayonnaise
2 oz pineapple chunks
3—4 oz grapes
2 stalks celery
4 large apples
1 level teaspoon grated lemon rind
2 tablespoons slivered almonds

1 roasting chicken
½—¾ pints chicken stock made from
    giblets (or chicken bouillon cube
    and water)
3 oz butter
2 slices fat bacon
3—4 sprigs parsley
1 bunch tender asparagus (or 1 tin
    green asparagus spears)
½ pint mayonnaise
2 liquid oz double cream
2—3 oz cooked peas, chopped beans or
    sweetcorn (optional)
¼ teaspoon paprika

Chicken Stuffed Apples

1. Make mayonnaise as in *Smoked Turkey Salad* (see p. 9). Add lightly beaten cream and season to taste.

2. Dice chicken finely and mix with drained pineapple chunks, peeled seeded grapes and chopped celery. Mix with mayonnaise.

3. Polish apples and cut in half. Scoop out flesh with a grapefruit knife or spoon. Remove core and dice remaining apple; add to mayonnaise.

4. Fill the apple halves with chicken mayonnaise. Sprinkle top with grated lemon rind and lightly browned almonds.

Chicken and Asparagus Mayonnaise

Cold chicken and asparagus with delicately flavoured mayonnaise, arranged on endive salad, suitable for buffet or summer lunch (Serves 4—6, cold)

1. Cook chicken as in *French Roast Chicken* (see p. 19) or buy ready cooked chicken. Remove meat from bones and cut into cubes.

2. Trim asparagus and cook in boiling salted water until tender and drain, or open tin of green asparagus spears and drain carefully.

3. Make mayonnaise as in *Smoked Turkey Salad* (see p. 9)

4. Mix chicken and mayonnaise. Add a little cream and peas, beans or sweetcorn, if available. Arrange in centre of a lettuce or endive-lined dish and place asparagus around edge in little bundles. Sprinkle top of chicken mound with paprika, and serve with crusty French bread and butter.

CHICKEN: EVERYDAY DISHES

Chicken and Ham Pie

Tasty pie of chicken, ham, mushrooms and onions, in a well flavoured sauce under a light pastry crust (Serves 4–6, hot or cold)

1 chicken weighing 3 pounds
4 onions
2 carrots
3 stalks celery
several parsley sprigs
1 bay leaf
6 peppercorns
2½ oz butter
3 oz mushrooms
1 oz flour
½–¾ pint strong chicken stock
2 level tablespoons mixed chopped
    parsley, thyme, tarragon
a pinch of mace
6 medium thick slices ham
1 package frozen puff pastry
1 egg

Pre-heat oven to 450°F Mark 7

1. Cut meat off chicken bones in large chunks. Put carcass and giblets in pan with 2 onions, carrots, celery, herbs and peppercorns. Cover with water and cook until well flavoured; strain and add salt.

2. Melt 1 oz butter, cook 2 thickly sliced onions for 3–4 minutes. Then add mushrooms; cook for 1 minute, remove and keep warm. Heat another 1 oz butter and fry chicken pieces in pan for 4–5 minutes to seal meat. Sprinkle in flour, then pour on stock and bring to boil, stirring constantly. Simmer for 1 minute. Then add onions and mushrooms. Sprinkle in herbs and seasoning.

3. Chop ham and make a layer at bottom of pie dish. Spoon in half chicken mixture, another layer of ham, remaining chicken mixture, and top with ham. Allow to cool.

4. Roll out pastry, place thin strip around moistened edge of pie dish. Brush this strip with water and place the large piece of pastry on top. Crimp edges together; then cut off excess with sharp knife. Make 3–4 holes to allow steam to escape, decorate with pastry leaves and flowers. Brush pastry with beaten egg.

5. Bake in hot oven for 25 minutes to cook pastry. Cover pastry with damp greaseproof paper or foil. Reduce heat to 375°F or Mark 5 for another 20 minutes to cook chicken.

Oven Fried Chicken

Chicken pieces coated with egg and breadcrumb mixture, baked in the oven and served with piquant tomato sauce (Serves 4, hot)

4 chicken parts or quarters
1–1½ oz flour
a little paprika
1–2 eggs
4–6 tablespoons breadcrumbs
4 tablespoons butter

TOMATO SAUCE
1 oz butter
1 onion
1 clove garlic
½ oz flour
2 level tablespoons tomato puree
1 small tin tomatoes
½ pint stock
1 tablespoon chopped mixed herbs
6 peppercorns
strip of lemon rind
pinch of cayenne pepper
1 teaspoon sugar

1. Roll chicken pieces in flour seasoned with salt, pepper and paprika, brush thoroughly with beaten egg and roll in dried breadcrumbs. Put chicken in a well buttered ovenproof dish.

2. Pour melted butter over chicken, put into oven and cook for 30–35 minutes, or until pieces are crisp and brown.

3. Meanwhile, make tomato sauce: Melt butter, cook finely chopped onion and crushed garlic until golden. Sprinkle in flour and add tomato puree, tinned tomatoes and stock. Bring to the boil; simmer for 20 minutes adding herbs, peppercorns, lemon rind and a pinch of cayenne pepper. Strain sauce and add sugar. Season to taste.

4. Serve the chicken very hot with sauce and rice or mashed potatoes.

Persian Chicken Pilau

Chicken pieces fried in butter and cooked in an aromatic apricot cinnamon yoghurt sauce layered with rice and finished with almonds (Serves 4–6, hot)

4–6 chicken pieces about 2 pounds or more
2 tablespoons oil
3½–4 oz butter
1 large onion
4 oz dried apricots
½ level teaspoon cinnamon
grated rind of 1 lemon
1 carton natural yoghurt
12 oz long grain rice
2 tablespoons almonds

Pre-heat oven to 350°F Mark 4

1. Heat oil and 1 oz butter. When foaming, fry chicken pieces until golden brown. Remove and allow to cool. Cook sliced onion until golden in the same oil and butter. Add chopped apricots; sprinkle with cinnamon, lemon rind, salt and ground black pepper. Remove bones from chicken pieces and shred meat. Mix yoghurt and onion mixture and soak chicken in this while rice is cooking.

2. Cook rice in boiling salted water for 10–12 minutes. Drain and rinse with boiling water. Dry for a few minutes. Heat 1½ oz butter in thick pan or casserole, put half rice into pan and mix well with butter and seasoning. Spoon chicken mixture over rice, and put remaining rice on top. Sprinkle with salt and pepper.

3. Melt remaining butter and spoon over rice. Cover pan with cloth and lid, and cook gently for 15–20 minutes until all the flavours are blended; the cloth absorbs extra moisture. (This process can be done in the oven but cloth should not be used.)

4. Brown slivers of almonds, sprinkle on top of rice, and serve at once.

Brunswick Stew

Chicken stewed with potatoes, broad beans, tomatoes, onions and sweetcorn using a method originally devised for cooking squirrels (Serves 4–6, hot—see picture, p. 22)

1 stewing or roasting chicken, about 3–4 pounds
½ teaspoon salt
3 potatoes
1 large onion
1 small tin broad beans
1 small tin tomatoes (or 5–6 sliced fresh tomatoes)
1 level tablespoon sugar
2–3 oz sweetcorn
1 tablespoon ketchup or Worcestershire sauce
2 oz butter

1. Cut chicken into pieces and put in casserole with enough boiling water to cover; add a little salt. Simmer for about 45 minutes.

2. Add sliced potatoes, sliced onion, broad beans, tomatoes and sugar to casserole. Cook for 45 minutes, when beans and potatoes should be tender.

3. Remove as many bones as possible from chicken, add sweetcorn. Cook for 10 minutes. Then season to taste, and add ketchup or Worcestershire sauce if desired. Add butter and stir well.

Chicken Marengo

Chicken pieces cooked in wine, tomato and vegetable sauce, with a fried egg on fried bread (Serves 4, hot)

4 pieces frying chicken
6 liquid oz oil
2½ oz butter
1 rasher bacon
1 onion
1 clove garlic
3 carrots
2 stalks celery
1 oz flour
2 tablespoons tomato puree
4 liquid oz white wine or sherry
½ pint stock
1 bay leaf
several parsley sprigs
3–4 oz mushrooms
4 slices bread
4 eggs
1 tablespoon parsley chopped

Pre-heat oven to 350°F Mark 4

1. Heat 2 tablespoons oil and add ½ oz butter. When foaming, cook chicken pieces until golden brown. Place in casserole.

2. Fry bacon, finely chopped onion, crushed garlic, sliced carrots and celery for about 5 minutes. Sprinkle in flour and cook for 1 minute. Add tomato puree, wine or sherry and stock. Bring to a boil, add seasoning and pour over chicken pieces. Add herbs and sliced mushrooms. Cover casserole and cook in oven for about 1 hour.

3. After about 50 minutes, fry bread cut in rounds in remaining oil and ½ oz butter, and drain on paper towel. Fry eggs in 1½ oz butter and when cooked place on fried bread.

4. Serve chicken pieces on a hot dish. Boil up sauce and strain over chicken, reserving excess. Sprinkle top with chopped parsley. Place the fried eggs around the dish at the last moment, and serve.

Chicken Tetrazzini

Shredded boiled chicken served on a bed of spaghetti with a delicately flavoured wine sauce, topped with cheese and crisp browned almonds (Serve 4–6 hot—see picture, p. 28)

1 stewing chicken weighing about 3–4 pounds
2 onions
2 carrots
parsley, thyme and a bay leaf
½ pound spaghetti
3 oz butter
dash of garlic powder
2 oz flour
¼ pint white wine
6–8 mushrooms
3–4 tablespoons double cream
1½–2 oz grated Parmesan cheese
2 tablespoons dried breadcrumbs
2 tablespoons sliced almonds

Pre-heat oven to 400°F Mark 6

1. Cook chicken slowly in water with onions, carrots and herbs until tender. Let cool in stock, if possible, overnight. Then remove skin and bones, and cook these in stock until it is well flavoured and reduced to 2–3 cups.

2. Boil spaghetti in usual way and finish off in ½ oz butter flavoured with a little garlic powder. Place in fireproof dish and keep warm.

3. Make velouté sauce. Melt 2 oz butter, add flour and when blended add ½ pint chicken stock, bring to boil and cook for 2 minutes. Then add wine and simmer for few minutes.

4. Meanwhile, cut cold chicken into long strips, place in a mound on top of spaghetti, and sprinkle with salt and pepper. Cook sliced mushrooms in ½ oz butter for 2–3 minutes; then put on top of chicken.

5. Add cream to sauce; check seasoning. Spoon sauce over dish; then sprinkle the top with cheese and crumbs. Bake in oven for 10–15 minutes, until the dish is well heated, and the top brown and crisp. Lastly, sprinkle browned almonds over the top and serve at once.

Chicken Chop Suey

Chinese dish of chicken in a clear sauce with mushrooms, onions, celery, and bean sprouts, served with rice (Serves 4, hot—see picture p. 29)

1 chicken weighing 3 pounds
4 onions
2 carrots
1 bunch herbs
6–8 peppercorns
8 oz rice
3–4 stalks celery
6–8 mushrooms
squeeze of lemon juice
1 tin bean sprouts
2 tablespoons soy sauce
1 tablespoon cornflour

1. Boil chicken with 2 onions, carrots, herbs and peppercorns until tender. Let it cool in water. When cool, remove skin and bones, and boil up stock with these and a chicken bouillon cube to make a well flavoured stock.

2. Boil rice in usual way, drain well and keep warm in oven.

3. Cut chicken into large chunks and reserve. Slice 2 onions and celery, and put these to cook in a little of the stock until just tender, 8–10 minutes. Cook sliced mushrooms in a little stock and lemon juice for 3–4 minutes; add to chicken. Mix chicken with drained vegetables, add drained bean sprouts, soy sauce, seasoning and ½ pint of chicken stock.

4. Heat gently. Meanwhile, mix cornflour with ½ pint of stock, add this to chicken mixture. Heat until sauce thickens and serve with boiled rice.

Chicken Florentine

Pieces of fried chicken on creamy spinach with a cheesy topping (Serves 4, hot)

4 pieces frying chicken
2–3 tablespoons seasoned flour
3 oz butter
1 pound spinach
½ oz plain flour
3–4 tablespoons cream
pinch of mace and paprika
2–3 tablespoons grated Italian cheese
2 tablespoons breadcrumbs

Pre-heat oven to 400°F Mark 6

1. Roll chicken pieces in seasoned flour; then fry in 1½ oz hot butter until golden brown, about 10 minutes.

2. Cook spinach. Drain and chop. Add 1 oz butter. When melted, sprinkle in flour. Bring to a boil; then add cream and seasoning, with a dash of paprika. Pour this into buttered fireproof dish. Place chicken pieces on top.

3. Mix cheese and breadcrumbs together, and sprinkle thickly over top of chicken. Dribble remaining butter over the top. Cook in oven for about 25–30 minutes, or until the topping is crisp and brown.

Mexican Chicken

4 large chicken pieces
1½–2 oz flour
½ teaspoon salt
a large pinch of garlic powder
¼ teaspoon pepper
2 medium onions
2½ oz butter
2 tomatoes
2 liquid oz white wine
6–7 liquid oz chicken stock
2–3 oz raisins
2 oz pimento-stuffed olives
¼ teaspoon cinnamon
3 tablespoons slivered almonds

Pre-heat oven to 375°F Mark 6

Chicken pieces cooked in an exotic flavoured sauce with onion, tomatoes, raisins, olives and cinnamon, and served with rice (Serves 4, hot)

1. Roll chicken pieces in flour seasoned with salt, garlic powder and pepper. Remove and toss onion slices in the same flour.

2. Melt butter; when foaming, fry chicken pieces until golden brown, about 7–10 minutes. Remove; keep warm in an ovenproof casserole. Add sliced onions and chopped tomatoes to butter. Cook for 4–5 minutes. Then add wine, stock, raisins, olives, herbs and seasoning. Bring to the boil, and pour over chicken pieces. Put into oven for 35 minutes or until chicken is tender.

3. Sprinkle with cinnamon and stir in. Lastly, sprinkle over browned almonds and serve at once with plain boiled rice.

Chicken in White Wine Sauce

1 chicken 2½–3 pounds in weight
2–3 slices onion
3–4 parsley sprigs or 1 teaspoon dried parsley
a pinch of mace or nutmeg
6 white peppercorns
1 bay leaf
¾ pint white wine
¼ pint chicken stock
2 oz butter
1½ oz flour
2 teaspoons tarragon leaves
2 liquid oz double cream

Pre-heat oven to 350°F Mark 4

Tender chicken cooked in white wine and served in a creamy sauce, flavoured with wine and tarragon (Serves 4, hot)

1. Cut chicken into pieces and put into casserole with onion, parsley sprigs, mace, peppercorns and bay leaf. Add wine and stock and cook in oven for 35–45 minutes, until tender. Remove chicken pieces, put into serving dish and keep warm.

2. Boil liquid left in casserole for a few minutes to strengthen flavour, and reduce quantity. Melt butter, stir in flour and when smooth strain in ¾ pint of the liquid. Season, and add 1 teaspoon tarragon leaves and cream.

3. Spoon sauce over chicken and sprinkle top with remaining tarragon leaves. Serve at once, with rice or mashed potatoes.

CHICKEN: TASTY LEFTOVERS

Chicken Crisps

Creamy chicken and mushroom mixture on crispy fried bread squares making a delicious quick supper dish (Serves 4, hot)

8 oz cooked chicken chopped or diced
1 oz butter
1 oz flour
½ pint milk
8 mushrooms sliced
4 tablespoons stock
3 oz cooked peas or sweetcorn
5 thick slices of white bread
8 liquid oz oil
½ oz butter
1 tablespoon parsley chopped

1. Make cream sauce: Melt butter and blend in flour. Gradually add milk; when smooth, bring to the boil, stirring constantly. Boil for 3 minutes, then cool slightly.

2. Slice mushrooms and cook in stock for 3–4 minutes. Chop or dice chicken, and mix with mushrooms and cooked vegetables. Add mixture to cream sauce, season well, heat thoroughly, and keep warm.

3. Remove crusts from slices of bread, and with a small cutter cut 4 crescent shaped pieces from the fifth slice. Heat oil and add butter. When foaming, fry bread slices until golden brown on both sides. Also fry the 4 small crescents. Drain on paper towel.

4. Arrange the fried squares on a serving dish, spoon the hot chicken mixture on to the squares, and decorate with the crescents and chopped parsley.

Chicken and Cheesy Rice Ring

Cheese flavoured rice, baked in a ring mould and filled with creamy chicken and mushroom sauce with crisp topping (Serves 4—6, hot—see picture, p. 27)

12—15 oz cooked chicken (or chicken and ham)
3 oz butter
2 onions
12—14 oz cooked rice
1 egg
½ pint milk
5 oz grated cheddar cheese
2 level tablespoons mixed herbs chopped
½ teaspoon dry mustard
½ teaspoon paprika
4—6 large mushrooms
1 oz flour
½ Pint stock (or tin condensed chicken or mushroom soup)
a pinch of nutmeg
1 green or red pepper
2—3 tablespoons breadcrumbs

1. Melt 2½ oz butter and cook finely chopped onions for 4—5 minutes to soften, without browning. Remove half and put into bowl. Add rice to onion in bowl. Add beaten egg mixed with milk, 3—4 oz grated cheese and 1 level tablespoon herbs. Season with salt, pepper, dry mustard and half the paprika.

2. Butter a 7 inch ring mould and fill with rice mixture, packing it in well. Bake for about twenty minutes. When firm and cooked, remove from oven and turn out on a platter.

3. Meanwhile, prepare chicken sauce: Add sliced mushrooms to onion in pan and cook for two minutes. Remove from heat, add

Duck Paté (see p. 39)

flour, mix well; then add stock (or condensed soup). Blend well, bring to the boil, cook for few minutes and add diced chicken, remaining herbs and seasoning. Flavor with nutmeg.

4. Boil coarsely chopped pepper for five minutes, drain and add to sauce. Keep sauce warm to allow flavours to blend. Spoon hot sauce into centre of rice ring. Any excess can be re-heated and served separately.

5. Sprinkle top with remaining cheese and crumbs mixed, dot over the last spoon of butter and brown under grill for a few minutes or in hot oven. Sprinkle with paprika and serve hot.

Fried Goose with Apple Rings (see p. 48)

Chicken and Corn Croquettes

Creamy chicken and sweetcorn mixture cooked in crispy coating of egg and breadcrumbs (Serves 4, hot)

1. Make a thick cream sauce. Melt 2 oz butter and stir in 2 oz flour. Add milk and blend smoothly. Bring to boil and cook for several minutes to reduce quantity slightly.

2. Melt ½ oz butter, and cook onion and sweetcorn for 3—4 minutes. Add chicken meat, chopped parsley, lemon juice, mace and mix well. Add 6 liquid oz of sauce, season well. Let cool; then add 1 egg yolk. Spread mixture out on plate to cool and thicken.

3. Divide into 8 equal portions and form into rolls. Turn in 3 oz flour seasoned with salt and pepper until completely covered. Brush all over with egg beaten with oil. Then coat completely with breadcrumbs. (They can be left for up to 1 hour at this stage before cooking.)

4. Heat oil or fat until gently smoking, then lower 3—4 croquettes at a time into hot fat and cook until golden brown and crisp. Drain on paper towel, and serve at once with lemon quarters and a salad or green vegetables.

8—10 oz finely chopped chicken
2½ oz butter
5 oz flour
½ pint milk
1 teaspoon onion finely chopped
2—3 oz tinned sweetcorn
2 teaspoons parsley
1 teaspoon lemon juice
a pinch of mace
3 eggs
1 teaspoon oil
5—6 oz dried white breadcrumbs
fat for deep frying

Chicken Liver Risotto

Tender chicken livers cooked with savoury rice, garnished with grated cheese for extra flavour (Serves 4, hot)

1½ oz butter
1 small onion
1 clove garlic
6—8 chicken livers
4—6 mushrooms
8 oz rice
1¼ pints well-flavoured stock or water
     and chicken stock cube
2 tablespoons parsley chopped
4—5 oz grated cheddar cheese

1. Melt butter, and cook chopped onions and crushed garlic for a few minutes. Then add halved chicken livers and quartered mushrooms. Cook until the livers change colour and stiffen slightly.

2. Add rice, stir well into other ingredients. Pour on half of the stock, and add seasoning and parsley. Bring to boil; then add most of remaining stock. Simmer gently for about 20—30 minutes, stirring from time to time and adding remaining stock to moisten, if necessary.

3. Serve with grated cheese in a separate bowl.

Duck Stuffed with Apricots (see p. 42)
(see p. 42)

Fried chicken with unusual peanut butter sauce (Serves 4, hot)

1 chicken, 2½—3 pounds
2 tablespoons oil
2 onions
1 level teaspoon curry powder
2 tablespoons tomato puree
½ pint chicken stock
1 tablespoon mixed parsley and thyme
1 bay leaf

PEANUT SAUCE
6—7 tablespoons peanut butter
¾ pint chicken stock

Chicken with Peanut Sauce

1. Cut chicken into pieces, season with salt and pepper. Heat oil and brown chicken pieces all over. Remove and keep warm.

2. Cook sliced onion until tender. Add curry powder and tomato puree. Stir until smooth, add stock and bring to boil. Add herbs and seasonings. Pour over chicken pieces. Simmer until tender, about 1 hour.

3. Make peanut sauce: Mix peanut butter with stock and season. When smooth, pour over chicken, heat for 10—15 minutes, and serve with boiled rice.

Diced chicken and mushrooms in a delicious light pastry roll (Serves 4, hot)

6–8 oz diced chicken
1–1½ oz butter
1 small onion
3–4 oz mushrooms chopped
½ oz flour
2 liquid oz chicken stock
3–4 tablespoons cooked peas, sweetcorn or beans
1 tablespoon parsley chopped
1 level teaspoon tarragon chopped
1 medium package frozen puff pastry
1 egg

Pre-heat oven to 450°F Mark 8

Chicken Koulibiaca

1. Melt butter and cook chopped onion until tender, 3–4 minutes. Add chopped mushrooms and cook for 1 minute. Stir in flour, then add stock and bring to boil. Mix diced chicken into sauce, with herbs, seasoning and cooked peas, sweetcorn or chopped beans. Allow to cool completely.

2. Roll out completely thawed puff pastry into a rectangle and place on a baking sheet. Spoon cooled chicken mixture down the centre of one side of pastry rectangle. Brush edges of pastry with water, fold flap of pastry over top, seal edges and crimp to make a pretty edge. With a sharp knife cut 3–4 slashes diagonally across pastry to allow steam to escape. Brush the whole surface with beaten egg.

3. Bake in oven for about 30 minutes, until pastry is brown and done. Remove to serving dish and serve hot.

Delicious light and economical chicken dish suitable for both old and young (Serves 4–6 hot)

1 pound cooked chicken
6–8 oz fresh breadcrumbs
2 oz butter
1 oz flour
½ pint milk
a large pinch of ground mace or nutmeg
1 tablespoon parsley chopped
1 egg

Pre-heat oven to 375°F Mark 5

Kitty's Chicken Cream

1. Mince chicken and mix with fresh breadcrumbs.

2. Make cream sauce: Melt 1 oz butter and blend in flour. Add milk gradually. When smooth, bring to a boil, stirring constantly. Boil 2–3 minutes; add mace or nutmeg and herbs. Let cool slightly.

3. Add sauce to chicken mixture. Stir well, adding remaining butter and beaten egg. Season well. Put in buttered fireproof dish, allowing room for chicken cream to rise slightly, and cook in oven for 30–35 minutes.

DUCK

Duck Paté

Delicious paté made from duck, liver, pork, bacon and herbs mixed with brandy and egg, baked in slow oven and then pressed; suitable for buffet (Serves 6–8, cold–see picture, p. 35)

1 pound cooked duck
½ pound duck and lamb liver chopped
¼ pound lean raw pork or veal chopped
4—6 oz fat bacon chopped
1 onion
½ clove garlic
4 tablespoons breadcrumbs
1 small egg
2 tablespoons milk
1 tablespoon parsley and thyme chopped
2 teaspoon grated orange rind
2—4 liquid oz brandy
a pinch of mace
10—12 rashers streaky bacon
4 slices orange
½ tin consomme
½ oz gelatine
1—2 tablespoons brandy (or sherry)

Pre-heat oven to 325°F Mark 3

1. Mince livers, pork or veal, fat bacon, finely chopped onions and crushed garlic together. Mix in breadcrumbs, egg beaten with milk, chopped herbs, orange rind and brandy (or sherry). Add seasoning and mace.

2. With a knife stretch bacon rashers by scraping, and line a loaf or paté pan completely with them. Cut cooked duck into strips and sprinkle half into the loaf pan, season, then cover with half the meat mixture. Put in rest of duck, then remaining mixture. Fold over any overlapping pieces of bacon. Cover the whole pan carefully with foil. Put in a baking pan of water and bake in oven for 2—3 hours.

3. Half an hour before the paté is done, remove foil and place 4 slices of orange down the centre, re-cover, continue cooking. When done, remove from oven and allow to cool. Put a double layer of greaseproof paper on top and weights to press paté and make it firm.

4. Dissolve gelatine in half a tin of consomme, let cool and add 1—2 tablespoons brandy (or sherry). When nearly set, turn paté out on to wire rack and spoon jelly consomme over it. Leave to set. Serve on a salad lined plate with orange segments for flavour and colour.

Cold Duck Souffle

Delicious light souffle of minced duck mixed with cream sauce, sherry, whipped cream and egg whites topped with a layer of orange slices set in jellied consomme (Serves 4—6, cold)

12 oz cold duck minced
½ pint milk
1 onion
1 carrot
6 peppercorns
a pinch of mace
4 stalks parsley (or 2 teaspoons dried parsley)
1 sprig of thyme (or ¼ teaspoon thyme)
1 bay leaf
3 cloves
1 oz butter
1 oz flour
2 tins beef consomme
1—1¼ oz gelatine
3 tablespoons sherry
4 liquid oz double cream
2 eggs
2 oranges

1. Make cream sauce: Put milk into small pan with sliced onion and carrot, peppercorns, mace, herbs and cloves. Heat slowly for 20 minutes. Melt butter, stir in flour, strain on milk and bring to the boil, stirring constantly. Simmer for 3—4 minutes. Allow to cool.

2. Meanwhile dissolve ¾ oz gelatine in ½ tin consomme. Add 1 tablespoon sherry and the finely minced duck. Mix well.

3. When sauce is cool beat and mix into duck and jelly mixture. Season well, as the flavour dulls when cold. Put bowl into large bowl containing iced water and ice. Stir from time to time. When on the point of setting stir in whipped cream and whipped egg whites. Put into souffle dish large enough to leave a little space for orange garnish and jelly. Put in refrigerator to set.

4. Meanwhile prepare garnish: With a sharp serrated knife, remove peel, pith and skin from oranges; cut into wafer thin slices. In remaining consomme dissolve ¼—½ oz gelatine. When cool add 2 tablespoons sherry. sherry.

5. When souffle has set, arrange orange slices in overlapping layers on top and spoon over the setting consomme. Return to refrigerator to set jelly and serve with green salad and potato with mayonnaise.

Duck

Danish Christmas Duck

Duck stuffed with apples and prunes, roasted and served with a creamy gravy as traditionally eaten at Christmas in some Danish households
(Serves 6, hot)

1 large duck, 5 pounds or more
½ oz butter
1 pound apples
4—6 oz stoned prunes
grated rind of ½ orange
salt, pepper, sugar
2 tablespoons oil
¾ pint brown stock
2 liquid oz port or red wine (optional)
1 level tablespoon cornflour
2 liquid oz double cream

Pre-heat oven to 350°F Mark 4

1. Rinse duck out with cold water and dry thoroughly. Prick breast with a fork and rub over with butter and seasoning.

2. For stuffing, peel and thickly slice apples. Remove stones from soaked prunes. Mix both with some grated orange rind and a little salt and sugar. Stuff inside duck and sew up opening.

3. Heat oil in oven. When hot, add duck and baste thoroughly. Roast for 1¼—1½ hours, basting frequently, adding a little stock half way through cooking. Just before duck is done, pour off pan drippings and brown bird in slightly hotter oven.

4. Put duck on to serving dish and keep hot while making sauce. Skim fat off roasting juices and add remaining stock. Cook for a few minutes; add port or red wine (if available). Mix cornflour with a little cold water. Spoon a little hot sauce into cornflour, then return to pan and bring to the boil. Lastly, add cream and seasoning. Serve with red cabbage and browned potatoes.

Peking Duck

An exotic way of roasting duck on a spit while basting with a special sauce which gives crisp rich texture to skin of duck (Serves 4, hot)

1 tender roasting duck, 3—4 pounds
4—5 tablespoons honey
2 teaspoons wine vinegar
1½ tablespoons soy sauce
2 teaspoons sherry
1 orange
1 onion

Pre-heat grill or barbecue charcoal grill

1. Prepare special basting sauce: In a pan put honey, vinegar, soy sauce, sherry, juice of ½ orange and 2½ tablespoons water. Heat all these ingredients together and bring to boil. Allow to cool.

2. Prick skin of duck lightly with a sharp fork, pour over several pints of boiling water to soften skin. Dry. Put onion and ½ orange inside duck and season. Put bird on spit and when grill or barbecue is very hot cook bird, basting frequently with special sauce. Allow 20 minutes per pound and lower heat after first half hour. Test if duck is done by sticking skewer deeply into leg meat. If juice is clear, duck is done.

3. Remove from heat and serve with rice and bean sprouts.

Roast Wild Duck with Baked Oranges

Wild ducks roasted simply with butter, and served with oranges baked whole as a garnish (Serves 4, hot)

2 wild ducks, about 1½ pounds each
2 onions
4 stalks celery
2 tablespoons lemon juice
3 oz butter
1½ tablespoons oil
4 small oranges or mandarins
3 teaspoons sugar
¼ pint clear stock

Pre-heat oven to 400°F Mark 6

1. Put a quartered onion and some celery into each duck with a little lemon juice and seasoning. Rub breasts over with 1 oz butter; sprinkle with salt. Heat oil and 1 oz butter in roasting pan. When hot, put in birds, basting well. Roast in oven for 25—30 minutes, depending on size of birds, basting every 15 minutes.

2. Wipe small oranges or mandarins, rub skins with butter. Put them around ducks for the last 15 minutes of cooking time. The oranges should swell and burst.

3. Remove ducks, put on serving dish and keep warm. Make a hole in each orange, fill with a little sugar and arrange around the ducks. Skim fat from pan drippings and add stock. Boil for several minutes to reduce quantity and season to taste. Serve with a salad and crisp potatoes.

Wild Duck with Red Cabbage

Wild duck cooked on top of a dish of braised red cabbage, with onion apple and caraway seeds (serves 4, hot)

1 wild duck, 2–3 pounds
1 small cabbage, 1–1½ pounds
3 onions
2 tablespoons vinegar
2 tablespoons water
4 cooking apples
1 level teaspoon sugar
2 tablespoons oil
1 teaspoon caraway seeds
¼ pint stock
1 tablespoon parsley chopped

Pre-heat oven to 350°F Mark 4

1. First braise red cabbage: Shred cabbage very finely, discarding any hard stem. Chop onion and mix with cabbage. Put in well-buttered casserole. Add vinegar, water and seasoning. Cover and cook in oven for 1 hour. Add sliced apples and a little sugar. Cook for 15 minutes more.

2. Cut duck into 4 pieces. Heat 2 tablespoons oil and when hot brown pieces of duck all over. Remove and place on top of cabbage in casserole. Cook sliced onions in remaining oil until soft without browning. Sprinkle in caraway seeds and add a little stock. Add seasoning and pour over pieces of duck. Return to oven for 30–40 minutes, until tender.

3. Scrape onion mixture off duck and mix it well into red cabbage. Arrange duck pieces on top of cabbage and sprinkle with chopped parsley. Serve hot, with mashed potatoes and redcurrant jelly.

Barbecued Duck

Duck basted with a barbecue sauce, roasted or grilled over a barbecue grill or on a rotary spit (Serves 4–6, hot)

1 duck, 3–4 pounds
4–5 tablespoons oil
¼ teaspoon dry mustard powder
1 clove garlic
a large pinch of seasoning salt
1 level teaspoon sugar
a pinch of cayenne pepper
black pepper
1 onion
1 tablespoon Worcestershire sauce
3 tablespoons bitter marmalade
1–2 tablespoons ketchup
1 tablespoon honey
1 tablespoon vinegar
1 orange
3–4 tablespoons stock
1 oz butter

Pre-heat rotary grill (or charcoal grill)

1. Mix 2 tablespoons oil with mustard, crushed garlic, seasoning salt, sugar, cayenne and black pepper. Prick breast of duck and rub this paste all over. Fix duck on rotary spit or barbeque spit. Put an onion and lump of butter and some seasoning inside.

2. Prepare the charcoal grill or heat the rotary spit element to red hot. Start grilling duck, turning frequently if over charcoal. Allow 20 minutes per pound, basting with oil for first 45 minutes then frequently with sauce.

3. Mix 2 tablespoons oil with Worcestershire sauce, bitter marmalade (sieved), ketchup, honey, vinegar, grated rind and juice of orange, ground pepper and 3–4 tablespoons stock. Heat thoroughly and baste duck.

4. When duck is tender and brown all over, remove from spit. Serve hot with watercress and orange salad.

Duck and Green Pea Pancakes

PANCAKES
4 oz flour
1 egg
1 egg yolk
8 liquid oz milk
½ oz butter
oil for frying

FILLING
5–7 oz diced cooked duck
2 oz butter
1 onion
6–8 mushrooms
¾ oz flour
¼ pint strong stock
2–3 oz peas
1 tablespoon chopped parsley and thyme
3–4 tablespoons cream
2 tablespoons browned breadcrumbs
grated rind of 1 orange

Pre-heat oven to 350°F Mark 4

Remains of roast duck mixed with cooked peas in a thick, tasty sauce, rolled in light French style pancakes, topped with orange crumbs (Serves 4–6, hot)

1. Make pancakes as in *Turkey and Tomato Pancakes* (see p. 12).

2. Melt 1 oz butter, and cook chopped onion and mushrooms in covered pan for 3–5 minutes to soften. Stir in flour, blend well. Then add stock. When smooth bring slowly to boil and cook for a few minutes. Add diced duck meat, peas and herbs. Heat for few minutes. Add cream last. Keep warm while cooking pancakes.

3. Put a spoonful of filling in centre of each pancake and roll up. Arrange in overlapping row in ovenproof dish. Spoon over remaining melted butter and some breadcrumbs, mixed with a little grated orange rind. Heat for few minutes in oven and serve.

Roast duck stuffed with apricots, basted with honey and orange juice, and served with a sauce laced with apricot brandy (Serves 4—6, hot, see picture, p. 37)

1 roasting duck weighing 4—5 pounds
1 pound fresh apricots (or 1 large tin, drained)
1 orange
1 onion
2 tablespoons oil
2—3 tablespoons honey
½ pint stock made with duck giblets (or a chicken stock cube)
2—3 tablespoons apricot brandy

Pre-heat oven to 400°F Mark 6

Duck Stuffed with Apricots

1. Stuff duck with half the stoned apricots and 3 strips of orange zest (the thin outer skin of orange), finely chopped onion and seasoning. Prick skin of duck with fork to allow the fat to run out while cooking and season with pepper and salt.

2. Heat oil in baking pan. When very hot add duck and baste all over with oil. Roast in oven, allowing 20 minutes per pound. Half an hour before cooking is completed, spoon over the melted honey and juice of orange which will give the skin a shiny crispness. 10 minutes before end of cooking, add rest of apricots to pan to heat through and brown slightly. Remove duck to a warm dish, and remove stuffing to a bowl. Arrange roasted apricots around duck.

3. Pour off fat from roasting pan, add stuffing to it with stock and bring to boil, stirring all the time. When the sauce has a pleasant flavour, strain or blend in liquidizer. Return to heat and add apricot brandy. Serve at once with duck and apricots.

1 duck, 3½—4 pounds
2 tablespoons oil
1 oz butter
3 onions
12 small or 6 medium white turnips
½—¾ pint stock
salt, pepper and a pinch of mace
3—4 stalks parsley
1 sprig thyme
1 bay leaf
1 tablespoon parsley chopped

Pre-heat oven to 335°F Mark 3½

Duck with Turnips

Duck cooked in stock and vegetable sauce garnished with small white turnips (Serves 4—6, hot)

1. Prick breast of duck with a fork; then rub with salt and pepper. Heat oil and butter, and when foaming brown duck all over. Keep warm while cooking sliced onions to a golden brown and peeled turnips to colour outsides slightly. Pour in stock, add seasoning and herbs and bring to a boil. Then return duck to casserole and spoon sauce over it. Cook in oven for 1—1½ hours.

2. When tender remove duck and turnips to serving dish, skim off fat from sauce. Boil this for a minute or two and season to taste. Add chopped parsley and spoon around bird. Serve at once.

1 duck over 1 year old
3 onions
thinly pared zest or rind of 1 orange
thinly pared zest or rind of 1 lemon
2—3 tablespoons oil
3—4 carrots
3—4 stalks celery
1 small white turnip
1½ oz flour
1 teaspoon tomato puree
¾ pint brown stock
¼—½ pint cider or red wine
several stalks parsley
1 sprig thyme
1 small sage leaf
1 bay leaf

Pre-heat oven to 340°F Mark 3½

Braised Duck

An excellent way of cooking an older duck, braised in oven in a a rich brown vegetable sauce (Serves 4, hot)

1. Prick breast of bird all over with fork. Rub skin with salt and pepper. Put an onion inside bird with a few pieces of orange and lemon zest (thin outer skin of fruit). Heat oil and brown duck all over for 6—8 minutes. Remove and keep warm.

2. Now add 2 sliced onions, carrots, celery, and turnip to pan and brown slowly but thoroughly. Cool slightly, add flour and cook for 2—3 minutes. Add tomato puree, stock and cider or wine. Boil for 1 minute. Add parsley, thyme, sage leaf, bay leaf, and remaining orange and lemon zest.

3. Place duck in casserole, cover with sauce and braise slowly in oven for 2 hours, until duck is tender.

4. Remove duck and carve. Place pieces on a hot dish. Strain sauce and boil to reduce slightly, skimming off fat which rises to top. Season to taste, spoon a little sauce over duck, and serve the rest separately.

Braised Quails with Risotto (see p. 63)

Duck with Cherries

Duck roasted with stock and wine or Maderia, served with a rich brown sauce and red cherries, party fare (Serves 4—6, hot)

1 duck, 4—5 pounds
2 onions
4 stalks celery
1½ oz butter
2 tablespoons oil
2 small carrots
4—5 mushrooms
¾ oz flour
2 teaspoons tomato puree
¾ pint stock made with giblets (or chicken stock cube)
a few stalks parsley
1 bay leaf
¼—½ pint red wine (or Madeira or port)
1 pound fresh red cherries (or 1 tin)
1 orange
¼ teaspoon sugar

Pre-heat oven to 400°F Mark 6

1. Put 1 onion and 2 stalks celery inside the duck. Rub breast with ½ oz butter and sprinkle with salt and pepper. Heat 2 tablespoons oil or butter; when hot put duck into roasting pan and baste well. Put into oven and roast for 15 minutes per pound, basting every 15 minutes. This will not cook bird completely, allowing 20 minutes for it to be cooked in the sauce.

2. Meanwhile prepare sauce: Melt 2 tablespoons oil, add one finely chopped onion, 2 carrots, 2 stalks celery and mushrooms. Cook for 7—10 minutes, allowing vegetables to brown lightly, stir in flour, brown for 1 minute. Add tomato puree, stock made from duck giblets and herbs. Bring to boil; then simmer for 30 minutes. Strain, add seasoning, bring to boil again and skim off any impurities which rise to surface. Add half the wine (or Madeira or port) and heat again.

3. Carve duck and arrange pieces in covered casserole. Pour sauce over and cook in oven for 20 minutes.

4. Meanwhile, prepare cherries. If fresh, remove stones, if tinned, drain off juice and remove stones. Put into small pan with juice and grated rind of orange, ¼ pint red wine and a little sugar. Heat gently for 6—7 minutes.

5. When duck is cooked, arrange pieces on serving dish, spoon sauce over top and arrange cherries around edge of dish. Serve hot.

Pigeons stuffed with Orange Rice (see p. 52)
(see p. 52)

Roast Duck with Orange Salad

Succulent duck roasted with a coating of honey, stuffed with celery, onions and herbs, and served with an orange salad (Serves 4, hot)

1 duck, 3—4 pounds
2 onions
4 stalks celery
1 oz butter
1 tablespoon chopped parsley and thyme
1 orange
2—3 tablespoons oil
2—3 tablespoons melted honey
4 oranges
¼ teaspoon salt
¼ teaspoon sugar
½ teaspoon freshly ground black pepper
3 tablespoons salad oil
2 tablespoons lemon juice
½ pint red wine
½ pint chicken stock

Pre-heat oven to 400°F Mark 6

1. Slice onions and celery, cook for a few minutes in a little butter, and mix in herbs and seasoning, including grated rind of half an orange and the juice of a whole. Rub skin of duck with butter and season.

2. Heat oil in roasting pan. When hot, add duck and baste with hot oil. Roast for 20 minutes per pound, basting every 15 minutes. During the last half hour, baste with melted honey. The honey produces a marvellous shiny brown skin.

3. Meanwhile, prepare the orange salad: Remove thin orange skin from one orange with a peeler, cut into match like shreds. Boil for 3 minutes in water, drain, refresh under cold tap to restore colour, leave to dry. With a sharp serrated knife, remove pith and skin from oranges and cut in thin slices, place in overlapping circles in glass dish. Mix salt, sugar and pepper with oil, then add lemon juice. Spoon dressing over oranges and sprinkle orange shreds over top. Chill in refrigerator.

4. When duck is cooked, remove from oven and keep warm on serving dish. Pour off excess fat, and pour red wine and stock into roasting pan. Bring to the boil, and cook until well flavoured. Add seasoning. The gravy may be too sweet because of the honey, so a little lemon juice may be added.

Salmi of Duck

Duck partly roasted, then cooked in rich wine sauce, and garnished with heart shaped bread croutons spread with cooked duck liver (Serves 6, hot)

1. Heat 2 tablespoons oil and roast duck for 35 minutes with giblets, but not liver. Let it cool enough to handle. Then carve the breast off in two pieces. Remove legs and any other meat carefully, reserving any blood that runs out while carving. Break up the carcass bones and remove skin from carved joints. Put bones and skin in pan with giblets and any blood or juice from duck. Place meat in a covered dish and keep warm.

2. Make sauce: Heat 1 oz butter and cook onion until tender. Then brown slightly, add flour, stir well and allow to brown a little. Cool slightly, add tomato puree and stock, bring to the boil and add duck bones, skin etc., herbs and seasoning. Cover pan and cook for 30 minutes. Then strain and add ¼ pint port or red wine. Cook again for few minutes, season to taste.

3. Cook mushrooms in ½ oz butter, then add to sauce. Melt another ½ oz butter in same pan and sauté duck liver until tender, season and chop or pound as fine as possible.

4. Carve duck's legs into two pieces and breast into slices and arrange these on an ovenproof serving dish. Spoon sauce over meat and cover dish with lid or foil and bake in oven until legs are tender, 20–30 minutes.

5. Meanwhile, cut bread slices into heart shaped croutons. Heat oil and add ½ oz butter. When foaming, fry croutons until golden brown all over. Drain and spread with duck liver paste.

6. When salmi is cooked, remove lid and sprinkle with chopped parsley and arrange croutons around the edge of the dish.

1 duck, 4–5 pounds
½ pint oil
2½ oz butter
1 onion chopped
¾ oz flour
1 level tablespoon tomato puree
¾ pint stock
a few stalks parsley, a sprig of thyme
  and a bay leaf
¼ pint port or red wine
12 button mushrooms
6 slices white bread
1 tablespoon parsley chopped

Pre-heat oven to 400°F Mark 6

Goose stuffed with onion, apple and chestnut stuffing, roasted in hot oven (Serves 6—8, hot)

1 goose, 8—10 pounds
2 pounds chestnuts
¾ pint stock
6 apples
2 onions
1 goose liver
½ oz butter
4—6 oz breadcrumbs
2 tablespoons parsley chopped
1 tablespoon mixed thyme and
    marjoram
grated rind of ½ lemon
1 oz flour
4—6 tablespoons oil
1½ tablespoons redcurrant jelly
juice of ½ lemon
½—¾ pint cider or stock

Pre-heat oven to 400°F Mark 6

GOOSE & PIGEON
Continental Roast Goose with Chestnut and Liver Stuffing

1. Prepare stuffing: Put chestnuts in boiling water for 5—6 minutes or until skins will remove completely. Then cover peeled nuts with stock and simmer until tender. Drain and allow to cool. Reserve stock for moistening stuffing. Peel and chop apples, chop onions and cook for 3—4 minutes, then mix in chestnuts. Cook goose liver in butter and when firm, chop and add to stuffing with 4—6 oz breadcrumbs. Add chopped parsley, thyme, marjoram, lemon rind, salt and pepper. Mix together adding enough stock to make a moist but firm mixture.

2. Stuff goose and sew up opening. Prick goose all over lightly with sharp fork, sprinkle with ½ oz flour and seasoning. Heat oil or fat in roasting pan. Put goose into pan, on a rack if possible to allow the fat to drain, and cook for 20—25 minutes per pound, basting every 20 minutes, turning from side to side. Reduce heat slightly after first 20 minutes. For last 30 minutes pour off most of fat, place bird breast up and allow to brown, raising heat again if breast is not becoming crisp and brown. Test with skewer in thick part of leg to see whether cooked. When cooked, remove to serving dish and keep warm while making gravy. *(cont.)*

3. Skim off any remaining fat from roasting pan, sprinkle in ½ oz flour and blend with roasting juices in pan. Add redcurrant jelly and lemon juice; stir in well. Add cider or stock and bring to boil. Cook for 2—3 minutes, strain, season to taste and serve hot with goose.

Roast Goose with Sage and Onion Stuffing

Goose stuffed with sage flavoured onion, apple and crumb stuffing, roasted in hot oven and served with gravy and apple sauce; a Christmas dish (Serves 6—8, hot)

1 young goose weighing 8—10 pounds
3—4 oz butter
2 pounds onions
8—9 fresh sage leaves (or 2 teaspoons powdered dried sage)
2 large cooking apples
10—12 oz fresh white breadcrumbs
grated rind of 1 lemon
1 egg
¾ pint strong stock made from giblets of goose (or chicken stock cube)
3—4 tablespoons oil
1 teaspoon flour
a little cider
1 large tin apple sauce

Pre-heat oven to 400°F Mark 6

1. Prepare stuffing: Melt butter and cook sliced onions slowly for 10—15 minutes without browning, stirring frequently. If using fresh sage leaves, dip these into boiling water for 1—2 minutes, drain and chop. Peel and chop 1 apple and mix with breadcrumbs, add chopped (or dried) sage, and lemon rind. Mix in softened onions, beaten egg and a few spoons stock. Season well with salt and pepper.

2. Wipe goose thoroughly inside and out. Weigh and calculate cooking time, allowing 20—25 minutes per pound. Fill cavity inside with stuffing allowing roughly 1 teacup per pound weight of bird. Sew up opening. Prick breast over lightly with a sharp fork to allow fat to run while cooking. Heat oil in oven, and when hot, put goose into roasting pan on a rack if possible. Baste well with hot oil. Season with salt and pepper. Put into oven and cook for 20—25 minutes per pound basting every 20 minutes. Reduce heat to 350°F Mark 4. During the last half hour put a sour cooking apple into roasting pan, as this gives the gravy a pleasant tang. If goose does not have a nice brown crisp skin at last basting, increase heat to 400°F for last 20 minutes. Remove bird when cooked and keep hot while making gravy.

3. Pour off all fat from roasting pan and sprinkle in flour. Add stock and bring to the boil, mashing roasted apple into sauce; a little cider may be added in place of some stock. Strain gravy into sauce boat, and serve apple sauce separately.

Potted Goose

A rich and delicious paté of goose liver and remains of roast goose pounded with butter and herbs; suitable as a first course or for a buffet party (Serves 6—8, cold)

1 goose liver
1—1½ pounds cold goose chopped
¾—1½ pounds butter
1 onion
1 clove garlic
2—3 tablespoons brandy or sherry
1 tablespoon chopped parsley and thyme
a large pinch of powdered mace (or slightly less nutmeg)

Pre-heat oven to 300°F Mark 2

1. Melt 1 oz butter and cook chopped goose liver until it has changed colour and stiffened. Remove and cool. Add 1 more oz butter and soften chopped onion and crushed garlic for 6—8 minutes without browning. Mix in herbs; add to liver.

2. Chop cold goose meat finely and mix with liver mixture. Pound together until smooth or put into liquidizer to mince finely, adding a little brandy or sherry if mixture seems to stick.

3. Weigh the resulting paté and for each pound add 8 oz softened butter. Season with powdered mace or nutmeg, salt and pepper. Beat together to mix thoroughly. Pack into a thick ovenproof mould. Cover with lid, heat through in oven for 15—20 minutes. Remove and cover with layer of unsalted butter. This helps the potted goose to keep longer.

4. Serve with lots of toast or hot French bread and butter.

Goose en Daube

Classic French method of cooking wild or domestic goose with wine, brandy, bacon, shallots or onions, garlic and herbs in slow oven; served cold in jellied sauce (Serves 6–8, cold)

1 goose, wild or domestic
3–4 oz bacon diced
4 oz shallots or mild onions chopped
2 cloves garlic
several stalks parsley
a sprig of thyme
2 sprigs basil (or ½ teaspoon dried basil)
1 large or 2 small bay leaves
2 cleaned and washed pig's trotters
    if available (or ½ oz gelatine added
    after cooking)
2 liquid oz brandy
½–1¼ pints red wine
¾ pint water or more if necessary to
    cover bird
3–4 tablespoons flour mixed to a
    thick paste for sealing casserole

Pre-heat oven to 300°F Mark 2

1. Put goose into a thick fireproof casserole with lid, on top of a layer of mixed bacon, onion and all other ingredients, sprinkling the rest over the top. Pour in all liquids, which should cover bird. Cover with lid and seal this with a paste made from flour and water. Cook in oven for about 4½–5 hours.

2. When dish has cooled, break seal and remove goose. Carve all meat and put slices in a large dish. Strain cooking liquid off all pieces of vegetables etc; skim off any fat, and check seasoning. If no pig's trotters were included, dissolve ½ oz gelatine in hot liquid. Pour this liquid over goose and put in refrigerator to set.

3. Serve cold with endive and orange salad, and hot potatoes.
(This method can also be used to cook duck or chicken but cooking time is shorter.)

Fried Goose with Apple Rings

Slices of cooked goose fried in egg and breadcrumbs, garnished with fried apple rings, served with a piquant sauce (Serves 4, hot—see picture, p. 36)

8 slices cooked breast of goose
2–3½ oz flour
1–2 eggs
¼ pint oil
4–6 oz fresh white breadcrumbs
2–2½ oz butter
2 cooking apples
1 level tablespoon sugar
½ pint brown gravy or sauce
1 tablespoon white vinegar
2 teaspoons Worcestershire sauce

1. Cut 8 thin slices of goose from breast of cooked bird. Season well. Cover well with flour, then dip in egg beaten with a little oil until completely coated. Then cover with dried white breadcrumbs.

2. Heat remaining oil and when hot add butter. When foaming, cook slices of goose until golden brown and crisp all over. Remove, drain and keep warm.

3. Peel, core and slice apples into 8 rings. Reheat fat in which goose was fried having removed any loose crumbs which may burn. Fry apple rings until golden brown, sprinkling each side with sugar to brown.

4. Make sauce by adding 1 tablespoon wine vinegar and 2 teaspoons Worcestershire sauce to brown gravy. Heat and season to taste.

Roast pigeons with savoury rice, almond and raisin stuffing (Serves 4, hot)

4 tender pigeons
4–6 oz cooked rice
2 onions
1½ oz butter
2–3 tablespoons peeled flaked
    almonds
1 tablespoon chopped herbs
3 tablespoons raisins
2–3 tablespoons sherry
4 slices fat bacon
2–3 tablespoons oil
1 teaspoon flour
¼ pint red wine
¼ pint stock

Pre-heat oven to 400°F Mark 6

Pigeons Stuffed with Almonds and Raisins

1. Prepare stuffing: Boil rice until tender. Drain and let it cool. Chop 2 onions and cook until soft in 1½ oz butter. Add skinned sliced onions and cook until all are golden brown. Add 8 tablespoons rice to pan, cook for 1 minute; then remove. Add chopped herbs, raisins which have been soaking in sherry and seasoning. Stuff mixture into pigeons.

2. Tie a slice of fat bacon around breast of each bird. Heat oil in oven, add pigeons and baste thoroughly. Roast in oven for about 35–40 minutes, basting and turning every 10 minutes. Remove bacon for last 15 minutes to brown breast. Remove to a serving dish and keep warm.

3. Pour away oil and sprinkle in flour, blend into pan drippings and add wine and stock. Stir until smooth and boiling, add seasoning and pour into sauce boat.

Cassoulet of Goose

A homely dish suitable for a cold winter's night; goose stewed with beans, garlic sausage, onions, tomatoes and stock; excellent way of using leftovers (Serves 4–6, hot)

2–3 pounds cooked goose joints
½–¾ pound dried broad beans (medium sized, or they will need longer cooking)
1¼–1½ pints strong brown meat stock (or water and beef stock cubes)
2½–3 oz goose fat (or butter)
2 medium onions
2–3 cloves garlic
4–5 slices fat smoked bacon
3–4 tablespoons tomato puree
1 tablespoon chopped parsley and thyme
a pinch of sage
1 bay leaf
6–8 slices garlic sausage
4–6 oz dried white breadcrumbs

Pre-heat oven to 300°F Mark 2

1. The day before you cook cassoulet put beans to soak. Next day put them in pan with water and bring slowly to the boil, lower heat and simmer for 2½ hours. Drain.

2. While beans cook, prepare stock: Cut goose into portions, add carcass to cooking stock to add flavour, and simmer until required. Melt 1–1½ oz of fat in which goose was roasted. Add sliced onions, crushed garlic and chopped bacon; cook for 5–6 minutes. Add tomato puree, herbs and seasoning. Add the drained stock. Bring to the boil, and simmer for 30 minutes.

3. Add drained beans to stock ingredients and stir well. Then pour half this mixture into bottom of thick casserole. Put in pieces of goose; then pour remaining bean mixture over top. Add sliced garlic sausage and submerge under liquid. Bring to a boil, add more seasoning if necessary, then sprinkle thick layer of breadcrumbs all over surface. Dot surface with 1 oz butter or goose fat. Put into oven and cook for about 1 hour, until beans have cooked and top is crusty and brown.
(This recipe can also be used for duck or turkey leftovers.)

Pigeon and Bacon Brochettes

Breast meat of pigeons marinated in wine and herbs grilled on skewers with bacon rolls, mushrooms and baby onions, served with a brown sauce (Serves 4, hot)

2–3 pigeons
¼ pint red wine
2 onions
1 level tablespoon chopped herbs
6 rashers bacon
8–12 baby onions
½–¾ pint stock
8–12 baby mushrooms (use stems for sauce)
3 tablespoons oil
1 clove garlic crushed
2 carrots chopped
2 stalks celery
1 oz flour

Pre-heat grill

1. Remove breasts from pigeons and cut each into 2 pieces. Put into bowl and cover with wine, one chopped onion, herbs and pepper. Allow to marinate for a few hours.

2. Cut 4 bacon rashers in half and make each into a roll. Cook peeled baby onions in ¼ pint stock for 5 minutes, drain and reserve stock for sauce. Peel mushrooms, remove stems and reserve for sauce. Remove pieces of pigeon from marinade and dry. Thread these ingredients alternately on to skewers.

3. Make brown sauce; Heat oil and cook 2 chopped rashers bacon, one chopped onion, crushed garlic, chopped carrots, chopped celery stalks and mushroom stems until they are golden brown. Sprinkle in 1 oz flour, blend well and add stock and ¼ pint strained marinade. Bring to boil and simmer for ½ hour. Strain and add seasoning.

4. Heat grill and cook brochettes, brushing with butter or oil, for about 8 minutes depending on heat of grill. The pigeon must not be overcooked as it becomes tough and tasteless if allowed to do so.

5. Serve with boiled rice, brown sauce and a salad.

Pigeons in Parcels

Halved pigeons pre-cooked slightly, then covered with a mushroom and paté mixture, wrapped in parcels of foil and baked in oven (Serves 4, hot)

2 large pigeons
3½–4 oz butter
2 rashers bacon
1 small tin goose or duck liver paté
4 oz mushrooms
1 tablespoon chopped parsley,
    marjoram and tarragon
a pinch of mace
1 tablespoon sherry

Pre-heat oven to 350°F Mark 4

1. Cut each pigeon in half and brown all over in 3 tablespoons butter with bacon. Cover dish and roast in oven for 20 minutes. Remove pigeons and allow to cool.

2. Mix paté with chopped mushrooms, 2 oz butter, chopped mixed herbs, seasoning and a dash of sherry. Cut 4 large squares of foil, butter these, place 1/8 of stuffing in the centre of each square. Place the halved pigeons on top; then spread another 1/8 of mixture over each pigeon. Fold the foil over the birds and seal edges by turning over several times.

3. Turn oven up to 400°F Mark 6 and bake parcels for 35 minutes. Serve a parcel per person, and open them at the table to get the full effect of the aroma.

Braised Pigeons with Red Cabbage

Tender pigeons braised in casserole with red cabbage and apples (Serves 4–6, hot)

2–3 large plump pigeons
4 oz butter
8 rashers bacon
3 onions
1 small or ½ large red cabbage
½–¾ pint strong stock
1 teaspoon sugar
1 tablespoon vinegar
4 cooking apples
2 liquid oz red wine

Pre-heat oven to 350°F Mark 4

1. Melt 3 oz butter in casserole and brown pigeons all over; remove and keep warm. Cook diced bacon, add sliced onions and brown. Then add thinly sliced red cabbage. Cook for 1 minute; then return the pigeons to pan. Pour over stock. Add salt, pepper, 1 teaspoon sugar and vinegar. Cover casserole, and cook in oven for 45 minutes.

2. Then remove casserole from oven, and add 2 sliced apples and wine. Cook again for 30 minutes; then remove pigeons and if cabbage is not quite cooked, simmer again until tender, keeping pigeons warm.

3. Cut pigeons in half, and lay on top of red cabbage. Fry remaining apples cut in rings in 1 oz butter and a sprinkling of sugar, and put one ring on top of each pigeon. Serve with a brown gravy.

Braised Pigeons with Mushroom Stuffing

Pigeons stuffed with mushroom and bread stuffing, braised in bacon flavoured brown sauce (Serves 4, hot)

4 pigeons
3 onions
1–1½ oz butter
2–3 oz mushrooms sliced
2 oz fresh white breadcrumbs
2 tablespoons oil
4 rashers bacon
½ pint stock
¼ pint red wine
1 tablespoon parsley and thyme
1 bay leaf
1 tablespoon parsley chopped

Pre-heat oven to 350°F Mark 4

1. Chop 1 small onion and cook for 3–4 minutes in butter; slice mushrooms and cook until tender. Add breadcrumbs, salt and pepper. Fill pigeons with this mixture.

2. Heat oil in casserole and cook chopped bacon until golden; remove and keep warm. Now brown pigeons all over in the hot oil. Remove and keep warm while cooking remaining chopped onion for a few minutes until golden brown. Add bacon; put back pigeons. Pour over stock and red wine. Add herbs and pepper, cover with lid and cook in oven for about 1 hour, until tender.

3. When cooked, remove birds and keep warm; skim fat from casserole. Boil sauce and season to taste. Serve birds in the sauce, sprinkled with chopped parsley.

Pigeon and Steak Pie

Lean steak and pigeon joints cooked with small onions and mushrooms in a savoury sauce, topped with a puff pastry, or browned mashed potatoes as topping. This dish is best if meat is cooked day before dish is to be eaten (Serves 4–6, hot)

1 pound lean steak
2 tender pigeons
1 onion
12 baby onions
4 oz mushrooms
2–3 tablespoons oil
1 oz flour
½ pint stock
¼ pint cider or beer
1 tablespoon mixed chopped parsley and thyme
1 bay leaf
1 tablespoon mushroom ketchup or Worcestershire sauce
1 package of frozen puff pastry (or 2 cups of potato mashed with butter and milk)
1 egg

Pre-heat oven to 325°F Mark 3 for cooking meat
Pre-heat oven to 425°F Mark 7 for pastry
Pre-heat oven to 400°F Mark 6 for potato topping

1. Cut lean steak into cubes. Cut pigeons into quarters. Chop onion and peel baby onions. Quarter mushrooms.

2. Heat oil, brown meat cubes and pigeons until brown all over, and remove to pie dish or casserole. Brown chopped onion and baby onions until golden brown, adding mushrooms after a few minutes. Stir in flour away from heat and blend, and add stock (or water) and cider or beer. Bring to boil; then add herbs, bay leaf, meat and pigeons. Cover with lid or foil, and cook in oven for 1–1½ hours, until meat is tender.

3. Allow to cool, if possible overnight. Skim off any surplus fat. Add more seasoning if needed and a little mushroom ketchup or Worcestershire sauce to give a lively flavour.

4. Roll out pastry thinly and cut a strip to go around edge of dish. Stick this to dish with water. Moisten top of pastry strip with water; then place large sheet of pastry over whole dish. Press edges together and cut off excess with a sharp knife. Crimp edges and cut air vents in pastry crust. Decorate with pastry leaves. Brush whole top with beaten egg. (If not using pastry, mashed potatoes can be used as a topping.)

5. Pre-heat oven to 425°F and bake pie for 20–30 minutes until pastry is crisp and brown. (If using mashed potatoes, heat oven to 400°F and brown for 15–20 minutes.)

Pigeons Stuffed with Orange Rice

Pigeons roasted with stuffing of rice, orange rind and segments and peeled grapes (Serves 4, hot—see picture, p. 44)

4 tender pigeons
6–8 oz rice
3 oranges
2–3 oz seedless grapes
a little powdered onion
2–3 tablespoons oil
1–2 teaspoons flour
¼ pint white wine

Pre-heat oven to 400°F Mark 6

1. Prepare stuffing: Cook rice and let cool. Grate rind of 1 large orange, mix with 8–9 tablespoons cooked rice. Remove pith and skin from 2 oranges with a serrated knife and cut out segments; add these to rice. Dip grapes into boiling water for few seconds, then into cold, peel and add to stuffing with salt, pepper and little powdered onion. Stuff mixture into pigeons.

2. Roast birds as in *Pigeons Stuffed with Almonds and Raisins* (see p. 48)

3. Pour away oil and sprinkle in flour, blend with pan drippings and add wine and a little stock. Bring to a boil and simmer for 1 minute. Add juice of 1 orange and a few strips of rind, and serve with the pigeons.

PHEASANT & GUINEA FOWL

Hot Pheasant Souffle

Delicious light concoction of eggs and minced pheasant (Serves 4, hot)

1. Melt butter, sift in flour and blend smoothly; heat for a minute or two, then add seasoned milk. Blend thoroughly and bring to the boil, stirring constantly. When boiling cook for 1 minute, then remove from heat and allow to cool. *(cont.)*

4–6 oz cooked pheasant
1¼ oz butter
1 oz flour
½ pint milk seasoned with onion,
   peppercorns, mace, parsley and bay
   leaf
a large pinch of onion powder
1 level tablespoon mixed herbs
a pinch of mace (or nutmeg)
3 eggs

Pre-heat oven to 325°F Mark 3

2. Chop or mince pheasant meat. Add to sauce, with onion powder and mixed herbs. Season highly, adding mace or nutmeg. Stir in beaten egg yolks. Allow mixture to get quite cool.

3. 35–40 minutes before you expect to eat souffle beat up egg whites with a pinch of salt. When very stiff fold in 1 tablespoon thoroughly, and then fold in remainder quickly, and lightly. Put into a 7 inch souffle dish and bake for 35–40 minutes until well risen. Serve at once.

1 guinea fowl large enough to feed 4
   or two smaller birds
4–5 oz mixed chopped onion, carrot
   and celery
3 stalks parsley
1 bay leaf
6 peppercorns
2 chicken stock cubes
4 oz mushrooms
1½–2 oz butter
1 teaspoon lemon juice
1½ oz flour
¼ pint white wine
4 liquid oz stock
4–5 tablespoons single cream
a pinch of mace

Guinea Fowl in White Wine Sauce

Guinea fowl cooked in stock until tender, then carved, covered with a white wine and mushroom sauce (Serves 4, hot)

1. Put cleaned guinea fowl in large pan with 4–5 oz mixed chopped vegetables, parsley stalks, bay leaf, peppercorns and 2 chicken stock cubes. Bring to the boil and cook gently until tender. Drain and carve, placing pieces in serving dish.

2. Cook quartered mushrooms in butter and lemon juice. Add flour and, when blended, the white wine and stock. Bring to boil slowly. Simmer for 2–3 minutes. Add cream and seasoning. Spoon over guinea fowl, and serve hot with rice or fried potatoes and a green vegetable.

PANCAKES
4 oz flour
1 egg
1 egg yolk
8 liquid oz milk
½ oz butter
oil for frying

FILLING
6—8 oz cold cooked pheasant meat
3—3½ oz butter
2 medium onions
8 mushrooms
1 oz flour
1 teaspoon tomato puree
a dash of Worcestershire sauce
6 liquid oz strong stock
2 tablespoons sherry
1 level tablespoon chopped parsley,
    thyme and marjoram
a pinch of nutmeg
2—3 tablespoons dry white
    breadcrumbs
2 tablespoons grated parmesan cheese
1 tablespoon parsley finely chopped
    or ½ teaspoon paprika

Pre-heat grill

Pheasant and Mushroom Pancakes

Delicious method of using up remains of cold pheasant with mushrooms heated in a tasty sauce and rolled in wafer thin pancakes (Serves 4—6, hot)

1. Make pancakes as in *Turkey and Tomato Pancakes* (see p. 12).

2. Melt 2—2½ oz butter and cook finely chopped onions until tender without browning. Add chopped mushrooms and cook for a few minutes. Sprinkle in flour, stir well and add tomato puree, Worcestershire sauce and stock. Bring to boil and simmer for 3—4 minutes. Add sherry and herbs, seasoning and nutmeg. Lastly, add pheasant meat, cut into shreds. Allow to heat thoroughly without boiling. Keep warm while making pancakes.

3. Put large spoonful of filling on each pancake and fold into triangle shape over filling or roll up. Place in an overlapping row down centre of ovenproof dish. Sprinkle with 2 tablespoons melted butter, then with breadcrumbs mixed with cheese. Grill until golden brown. Garnish with chopped parsley, or a sprinkling of paprika.

Pheasant Chasseur

Jointed pheasant browned in butter, then cooked in chasseur sauce (Serves 4, hot)

1 pheasant
2½ oz butter
2 oz mushrooms chopped
3 shallots or 1 mild onion
¼ pint white wine
2 teaspoons tomato puree
½ pint brown sauce (or strong stock)
1 level teaspoon tarragon chopped
1 tablespoon parsley chopped

Pre-heat oven to 350°F Mark 4

1. Make sauce: Heat 1 oz butter or 2 tablespoons oil, and brown chopped mushrooms for a few minutes, add chopped shallots or onions, cook for another minute. Add white wine and reduce liquid by half. Add tomato puree and brown sauce. Cook together for a minute or two, then add chopped tarragon and 1 tablespoon chopped parsley.

2. Joint pheasant and brown each piece in 1–1½ oz butter. Put into casserole and pour the sauce over. Cook in oven for 40–50 minutes until tender. Just before serving add a lump of butter to sauce. Sprinkle top with remaining parsley and serve hot.

Roast Pheasant

Tender young pheasant roasted in butter, served with a red wine gravy, fried breadcrumbs, bread sauce and game chips (Serves 4, hot)

1 young pheasant cleaned and drained
2–3 slices fat bacon
1 onion
3 oz butter
2–3 stalks parsley
½ pint chicken stock
½ pint red wine
1 pound potatoes
fat for deep frying

1. Tie slices of fat bacon over breast of pheasant; put onion and 1 oz butter with some seasoning and parsley stalks inside it.

2. Melt 1½–2 oz butter in roasting pan without burning. Place pheasant in roasting pan on rack and baste well. Pour on ¼ pint stock and ¼ pint red wine. Put bird in oven and cook for 40–60 minutes depending on size, basting every 15 minutes, and turning bird from side to side. For last 15 minutes, remove bacon and string, and allow breast to brown.

3. Remove bird and keep warm while making gravy. Pour off butter from roasting juices and add ¼ pint stock and ¼ pint red wine. Bring to boil, stirring constantly. Season to taste and after 3–4 minutes strain into a sauce boat.

4. Game chips are made from very thinly sliced potatoes, washed and dried carefully and fried in very hot, deep fat, a few at a time, until brown and crisp.

Roast Pheasant with Cream and Red Currant Sauce

Pheasant or other game birds roasted with red wine and butter, served with a sauce enriched with cream and sharpened with redcurrant jelly; a Scandinavian speciality (Serves 8, hot)

2 young pheasants
3½ oz butter
1 onion
4–6 slices fat bacon
½ pint red wine
½ pint single cream
2 tablespoons redcurrant jelly

Pre-heat oven to 400°F Mark 6

1. Put 1 oz butter and half an onion inside each bird and rub ½ oz butter over skin of each. Sprinkle with pepper and salt and cover with slices of bacon. Tie these on securely. Melt 1½ oz butter in roasting pan. When hot, put in birds and baste well with hot fat. Put into oven and roast for 45–60 minutes depending on size, basting every 15 minutes. After first half hour, pour wine over and baste. For last 15 minutes remove bacon and brown breasts well. When cooked, remove birds and make sauce.

2. Pour off all fat. Pour cream into the sauce left in pan and stir well. Then bring slowly to a boil, add softened red currant jelly and seasoning to sauce, strain into sauce boat and serve with pheasant.

3. Serve with game chips as in *Roast Pheasant* (see above) and watercress and orange salad.

Normandy Pheasant

Pheasant part roasted, part braised, on a layer of apples with a cream and apple brandy sauce (Serves 4, hot)

1 pheasant
3– 5 medium sized cooking apples
1 oz butter
½ pint double whipping cream
½ lemon
3–4 tablespoons apple brandy (optional)

Pre-heat oven to 425°F Mark 7

1. Put pheasant on to rotary spit if available or into a hot oven in a little butter and brown all over for 10–15 minutes. Remove and put into casserole which is lined with half the peeled, sliced cooking apples. Pour over any fat or juice from spit pan or roasting pan, and put remaining apples on top.

2. Put into oven at 350°F and cook for about 30–35 minutes. Then add cream and lemon juice, and apple brandy if available. Return to oven and cook for 10–15 minutes, until pheasant is tender.

3. Serve with the apple cream mixture as a thick sauce.

Pheasant a la Creme

Sautéed pheasant served on slices of toast, spread with cooked liver and covered with a cream sauce (Serves 4–6, hot)

1 large pheasant
4 oz butter
1 onion
1 level tablespoon chopped parsley
½ pint double cream
1 pheasant liver
1 large slice toast
1 teaspoon brandy (optional)
1 level teaspoon cornflour (optional)

1. Heat 3 oz butter. When foaming, brown pheasant on all sides. Add the finely chopped onion and herbs. Cover casserole with lid or foil, and simmer for 40 minutes, until pheasant is nearly cooked. Pour over cream and cook for 5–10 minutes.

2. Meanwhile, melt 1 oz butter and sauté pheasant liver until it has changed colour and stiffened. Remove from cooker and mash with seasoning and a teaspoon of brandy, if available. Spread on toast. When pheasant is done place on toast and keep warm.

3. If sauce seems rather thin and buttery, mix cornflour with 1 tablespoon cold water and add to sauce; heat gently until it thickens, season to taste, and pour over pheasant. Serve at once.

Braised Pheasant with Chestnut Puree and Orange

Pheasant braised in a well flavoured sauce, served on a puree of chestnuts garnished with segments of orange and orange rind; a good way of using an older bird (Serves 4–6, hot)

1 large pheasant
2–2½ oz butter
2 onions
2 small carrots
2–3 stalks celery
1 oz flour
½–¾ pint stock
¼ pint cider (or white wine)
3 oranges
1 tablespoon mixed herbs
1 large tin chestnut puree

Pre-heat oven to 350°F Mark 4

1. Melt 1–1½ oz butter in casserole. Brown bird slowly, all over. Remove bird and keep warm. Now add sliced onions, carrots and celery. Cook until they are beginning to brown slightly; add flour and cook for a few minutes. Add stock and cider or wine. Stir well and bring to boil. Simmer for a few minutes. Add 3 strips of orange rind, herbs and seasoning. Put the pheasant back into casserole and spoon sauce over it. Cover casserole and put into oven for about 50 minutes, until pheasant is tender. When pheasant is removed from casserole, boil up cooking juices and put into liquidizer. When smooth, return to pan and if too thick add a little extra stock. Season to taste and re-heat.

2. Meanwhile, melt 1 oz butter in pan and add chestnut puree. Heat, to soften puree, adding 2–3 tablespoons strong stock and seasoning. Keep warm until pheasant is tender; then place it down centre of serving dish. Place carved slices and joints on top. Spoon sauce over all.

3. Remove rind of orange carefully and cut into thin shreds. Cook in boiling water for a few minutes, drain and put in cold water to restore colour. Remove white pith and skin from oranges with sharp knife and divide into segments. Arrange orange segments around edge of dish and the orange strips down centre. Serve hot with fried or croquette potatoes, and a green vegetable.

Pheasant, Celery and Apple Casserole

Whole pheasant braised on a bed of onion, celery and apples with a white wine sauce, garnished with fried apple rings (Serves 4, hot)

1 pheasant
2—2½ oz butter
2 onions
3—4 stalks celery
2 medium sized apples
1—1½ pints chicken stock
¼ pint white wine
1 tablespoon mixed herbs
1 bay leaf
1 teaspoon sugar
1 tablespoon parsley chopped

Pre-heat oven to 350°F Mark 4

1. Melt 1—1½ oz butter in a casserole, add pheasant and brown slowly all over. Remove bird and keep warm. Slice onions, add to butter and soften for 5 minutes. Then add sliced celery, cook again for 2—3 minutes and add 1 sliced apple. Return pheasant and pour over stock and white wine. Sprinkle with salt and pepper; add herbs and bay leaf. Cover the casserole and cook in oven for 50 minutes, until bird is tender.

2. Remove pheasant to serving dish or carve into portions. Remove bay leaf, then put pan drippings and vegetables into liquidizer and blend until smooth. Re-heat, skim off any surplus butter that rises to surface. Season to taste, and pour over the pheasant.

3. Cut remaining peeled and cored apple into rings, sprinkle with sugar. Melt 1 oz butter and fry rings until golden brown. Place on top of dish, and sprinkle with chopped parsley.

American Pheasant

Pheasant split and flattened, sautéed in butter, covered with crumbs and grilled; served with broiled bacon, mushrooms and tomatoes (Serves 4, hot)

1 pheasant
4—6 oz butter
6—8 oz fresh white breadcrumbs
salt, pepper and a pinch of cayenne
    pepper
4 tomatoes
4 rashers bacon
8 flat mushrooms

Pre-heat grill to moderate temperature

1. Cut pheasant open along back with sharp knife. Open it out and flatten with a heavy rolling pin. Season with salt and pepper. Melt butter in large pan and when hot sauté pheasant on both sides. Remove from heat.

2. Make plenty of fresh white breadcrumbs and cover surface of pheasant with these; sprinkle with a little cayenne pepper. Heat grill and grill slowly so that the crumbs do not become too brown before bird is cooked. Test with skewer in thickest part of leg.

3. At the same time, grill halved and seasoned tomatoes. Also grill bacon, and mushrooms filled with butter and seasoned.

4. When pheasant is cooked, serve on a platter surrounded by grilled accompaniments and some butter balls rolled in parsley. Serve a salad with French dressing, separately.

Pheasant with Grapes and White Wine Sauce

Pheasant fried in butter then cooked in a white wine sauce, and garnished with white grapes (Serves 4, hot)

1 pheasant
2 oz butter
1 oz flour
¼ pint clear stock
¼ pint white wine
4—6 oz white grapes, seedless if
    available
2 tablespoons lemon juice

Pre-heat oven to 350°F Mark 4

1. Melt butter in casserole; when hot fry pheasant gently all over until golden brown. Remove bird. Add flour, stock and wine. Blend smoothly; then bring to the boil. Add seasoning. Return bird to casserole. Cover and cook in oven for 35—45 minutes, until pheasant is tender, turning over during cooking.

2. Peel grapes by dipping in boiling water for a few seconds and then in cold. Strip skins and if not seedless remove seeds. Cover with a little lemon juice to prevent browning.

3. When bird is tender, remove and carve. Place meat on a serving dish and keep warm. Add grapes to sauce and cook for couple of minutes. Season to taste and then spoon over the pheasant. Serve with mashed potatoes and peas or spinach.

American Braised Guinea Fowl

1 guinea fowl (or pheasant)
1½ oz butter
1 onion
1 clove garlic
¼ teaspoon dry mustard
2 teaspoons wine vinegar
6 liquid oz chicken stock
1 tablespoon chopped parsley and
tarragon
¾—1 pound cooked rice
1 teaspoon paprika

Pre-heat oven to 350°F Mark 4

Guinea fowl or pheasant cut in quarters and braised in a piquant sauce (Serves 4, hot)

1. Cut guinea fowl or pheasant into quarters and brown all over in butter. Add sliced onion, crushed garlic, mustard, vinegar, stock, chopped herbs and seasoning. Cover casserole and simmer on top of cooker or in oven for 30—35 minutes when bird should be almost tender. Remove lid and allow to simmer until liquid is much reduced, and bird is cooked through.

2. Boil rice and arrange in a ring around dish, spoon the guinea fowl into centre and sprinkle with paprika as garnish.

Roast Guinea Fowl

2 guinea hens
4—6 oz dry white breadcrumbs
8 oz butter
1 onion
2—3 oz mushrooms chopped
1 oz parsley chopped
2 tablespoons thyme and basil chopped
a pinch of mace
1 egg
a little milk
½ pint stock
a little white wine (optional)

Pre-heat oven to 350°F Mark 4

Young guinea hens stuffed with bread, mushroom and onion stuffing roasted to perfection in butter and stock (Serves 4, hot)

1. Prepare mushroom and herb stuffing: Put breadcrumbs in bowl. Melt 4 oz butter and cook finely chopped onion gently for 5 minutes without browning. Add mushrooms and cook for 2 minutes. Stir into breadcrumbs. Add parsley, thyme and basil. Season with salt, pepper and mace. Add beaten egg and enough milk to moisten without becoming runny. Allow to stand for a few minutes before stuffing into guinea hens. Sew up openings.

2. Rub breast and legs of guinea hens over with 1 oz butter. Sprinkle with seasoning. Melt 2—2½ oz butter (or 4 tablespoons oil) in roasting pan. When hot, put bird into pan and baste. Pour in ¼ pint stock. Roast slowly in oven, allowing 25 minutes per pound unstuffed weight, basting frequently and turning birds from side to side; but stand breast side up for last 30 minutes and turn up heat slightly to brown. When cooked, remove from pan and place on hot dish; keep warm. Pour off fat from roasting pan, add ¼ pint of stock and stir into pan drippings to make delicious gravy. (A little white wine can be added to gravy, if desired.)

Guinea Fowl Chasseur

1 large or 2 small guinea fowl (or 1
pheasant)
2½ oz butter
2—3 oz mushrooms chopped
3 shallots or 1 mild onion
¼ pint white wine
2 teaspoons tomato puree
½ pint brown sauce (or strong stock)
1 teaspoon tarragon chopped
GARNISH
4 rashers streaky bacon
2 large slices white bread
4—6 tablespoons oil
1—1½ oz butter
1 guinea fowl liver
1 teaspoon onion chopped (or a little
onion powder)
1 teaspoon sherry
1 tablespoon parsley chopped

Pre-heat oven to 350°F Mark 4

Guinea fowl or pheasant cut into pieces, browned in butter and cooked in chasseur sauce, garnished with bacon rolls and croutons spread with guinea fowl liver (Serves 4, hot)

1. Cook bird as in *Pheasant Chasseur* (see p. 55) except for garnish.

2. Make garnish: Cut bacon rashers in half, roll up and put on skewer. Grill or bake in oven until crisp. Cut bread into triangles. Fry these until golden brown in oil and butter. Drain; keep hot. Cook liver in 1 oz butter with a little onion and a teaspoon sherry. When cooked spread the mashed liver on to the croutons and arrange around dish alternately with the bacon rolls. Sprinkle with chopped parsley.

Turkish Guinea Fowl

1 guinea fowl
2–3 tablespoons oil
3 onions
several stalks parsley
1 bay leaf
8 peppercorns
1½–2 oz butter
1 clove garlic
8 oz rice
1–1¼ pints stock
2 oz raisins
½ teaspoon ground cinnamon
1 tablespoon herbs chopped
3 tablespoons almonds halved
1 tablespoon parsley chopped

Pre-heat oven to 325°F Mark 3

Guinea fowl simmered in stock until tender, then cooked with rice, almonds, herbs and raisins (Serves 4–6, hot)

1. Brown guinea fowl all over in oil. Then put into a large pan or casserole and barely cover with water. Add 2 sliced onions, parsley stalks, bay leaf, peppercorns and salt. Cook gently until tender, about 1½ hours. Drain and allow to cool, reserving stock for cooking rice.

2. Heat 1½–2 oz butter in pan, cook one chopped onion and crushed garlic until golden. Add rice and cook for a few minutes. Pour in 1–1¼ pints stock and bring to boil, add raisins and herbs, cinnamon and seasoning. Cut guinea fowl meat into good sized chunks and add to rice mixture. Cover dish and cook in oven for 20–30 minutes until all liquid has been absorbed and guinea fowl is tender. Sprinkle top with browned almonds and chopped parsley, and serve hot.

OTHER GAME

Grouse, Partridge or Pheasant Paté

Game mixed with liver, bacon and herbs to make a rich paté (Serves 6—8, cold)

2 grouse or partridges or 1 pheasant
½—¾ pound calf or chicken livers
6 rashers streaky bacon
2—3 oz butter (or bacon fat)
1 onion
1 clove garlic
2 level tablespoons chopped parsley,
    thyme and savory
1 bay leaf
2 oz flour
6 oz clarified butter

Pre-heat oven to 325°F Mark 3

1. Cut meat off birds and cut in slices, chop liver and bacon. Melt 1 oz butter (or bacon fat) and cook chopped onion and crushed garlic until tender. Add chopped bacon and liver, cook for a few minutes. Allow to cool slightly; then mince in liquidizer or pound in bowl. Add seasoning and chopped herbs.

2. Cook game pieces in 1 oz butter for 2—3 minutes. Then allow to cool. Arrange game and liver paste in layers in a thick casserole with a lid, making sure top layer is liver. Put a bay leaf on top. Cover, and seal with flour and water paste.

3. Put into deep baking pan of hot water, and cook in oven for 2½ hours. When cooked, remove lid and put several layers of greaseproof paper on top. Press down with weight and leave overnight. Either turn out and eat at once or pour layer of clarified butter over the top and keep in refrigerator.

A deliciously filling dish for using up cold, cooked game, in a rich sauce and served in a ring of savoury choux pastry (Serves 4, hot)

5 oz flour
4 oz butter
½ pint water
2 large or 3 small eggs
4 tablespoons grated cheddar cheese
¼ teaspoon dried mustard

FILLING
6–8 oz cold cooked grouse and partridge (or other game)
1 oz butter
1 onion chopped
6–8 mushrooms sliced
½ oz flour
1 teaspoon tomato puree
¼ pint stock
2 tablespoons sherry
1 tablespoon chopped herbs
2–3 oz cooked vegetables, as available
1 teaspoon Worcestershire sauce
2 tablespoons grated Parmesan cheese
2 tablespoons breadcrumbs
1 tablespoon parsley chopped

Pre-heat oven to 375°F Mark 5

Gougere of Grouse, Partridge and Mushrooms

1. Sift flour with a large pinch of salt and put in oven to keep warm. In a sloping sided pan heat ½ pint water and 4 oz butter. When butter has melted, bring to the boil. As soon as it boils, remove from heat and add flour all at once. Beat hard with a wooden spoon until mixture forms a ball in bottom of pan. Spread out on a plate to cool. Beat eggs. When mixture is cool, add egg by degrees, beating hard between each addition. Final mixture should be shiny and smooth, and will hold its shape. A little egg may be left over. Add cheese with mustard and seasoning.

2. Make filling: Melt butter and cook chopped onion for 5–6 minutes until soft. Add mushrooms, cook for 1 minute. Sprinkle in flour. When mixed in, add tomato puree and stock. Bring to the boil; cook for few minutes to thicken. Add sherry, diced game, herbs and any cooked vegetables such as peas, beans, sweetcorn or pepper, which are available. Add Worcestershire sauce. Allow to cool slightly.

3. Butter a fireproof dish about 3 inches deep. Arrange pastry in a ring around the outside of dish. Brush over with any remaining egg to give a shiny finish. Spoon filling into centre of pastry ring. Sprinkle the top with grated cheese and breadcrumbs. Bake in oven for 30–45 minutes. Sprinkle top with chopped parsley and serve.
(This recipe can be used for any other game.)

Hot Game Cutlets

Remains of game or turkey chopped and added to mashed potato, mixed with chutney, egg and herbs, fried in egg and crumbs (Serves 4, hot)

4—6 oz game
1 oz butter
1 onion
4—6 oz mashed potato
1 tablespoon herbs chopped
2 tablespoons chutney
1 egg
1½—2 oz flour
1—2 beaten eggs with 1 teaspoon oil
4—6 oz dry white breadcrumbs
fat for deep frying
tomato sauce

1. Chop 4—6 oz cold game. Heat butter and cook chopped onion until tender. Add to game with enough mashed potato to make a firm mixture. Add herbs, chutney, beaten egg and seasoning.

2. Mould into cutlet shapes, and when firm, roll in seasoned flour. Then brush with eggs beaten with oil and cover completely with dry white breadcrumbs.

3. Heat fat and fry cutlets for a few minutes, until golden brown, drain and serve with tomato sauce.

Cold Game Souffle

Minced game mixed with stock, gelatine, eggs and sherry to make a light cold souffle; suitable for cold buffet (Serves 4, cold)

8 oz minced cold game or turkey
¾ pint stock
¾ oz gelatine
2—3 tablespoons dry sherry or port
2 eggs
3—4 tablespoons double cream
cucumber and watercress for garnish
seasoning

1. Mince game. Dissolve gelatine in hot stock. Add to game with sherry or port. Beat egg yolks thoroughly and stir into mixture. Add seasoning.

2. When cold and almost set, add whipped cream and fold in beaten egg whites. Turn into souffle dish and allow to set. Keep cold in refrigerator.

3. Decorate with cucumber and watercress, and serve with a salad.

4 quails
4 vine leaves
1½ oz butter
2 onions
1 carrot
2 stalks celery
2—3 oz mushrooms
¼ pint stock
2—3 tablespoons sherry
1 tablespoon herbs chopped

RISOTTO
1 oz butter
1 onion
8 oz rice
1¼ pints stock
2 tablespoons raisins
1 green pepper
1 tablespoon herbs chopped
8—10 olives
2 tablespoons almonds

Pre-heat oven to 350°F Mark 4

Braised Quails with Risotto

Quails wrapped in vine leaves, cooked on a bed of vegetables, and served on a rich risotto with almonds, raisins, green peppers and olives (Serves 4, hot—see picture, p. 43)

1. Wrap quails in vine leaves and put a small piece of butter inside each one. Melt 1 oz butter, and cook sliced onions, carrot and celery, and chopped mushrooms until golden brown. Place quails on top of vegetables in an ovenproof dish and add a little sherry, 3—4 tablespoons stock, a sprinkling of herbs and seasoning. Put into oven and braise for 25 minutes, or until tender.

2. Make risotto: Heat butter and cook chopped onion until golden brown. Add rice and cook for 1 minute. Pour on stock and add raisins, chopped pepper and herbs. Put in moderate oven for 20—30 minutes or until rice has absorbed all liquid. Mix in olives and browned almonds, and serve on dish with the quails on top, and with a sauce made from the pan gravy and remaining stock and sherry.

2 partridges
1—1½ oz butter or bacon fat
2 onions
1 carrot
½ oz flour
½ pint stock
2 tablespoons parsley chopped
1 firm cabbage
8—10 rashers bacon
1 bay leaf

Pre-heat oven to 325°F Mark 3

Braised Partridges with Cabbage

Partridges cooked on a bed of bacon and cabbage with braising vegetables (Serves 4, hot)

1. Cut each partridge in half, and brown all over in 1—1½ oz butter or bacon fat. Remove and keep warm. Add sliced onions, carrot and cook until golden brown. Stir in flour, brown slightly, and add stock and chopped parsley.

2. Cut cabbage into quarters and remove hard core. Boil in salted water for 5—7 minutes, drain and allow to dry slightly.

3. Line casserole with bacon rashers and place half the cabbage on top with half the sauce. Then put partridges on top. Place remaining cabbage on top, and pour over rest of sauce. Put a bay leaf on top. Put on lid, and cook in oven for 1—1½ hours, until partridges and cabbage are tender.

4. Remove from oven and place partridges on top of cabbage to serve. Remove bay leaf.

2 grouse (or other game)
½ pound steak
½ pound streaky bacon
1 large onion
4—6 mushrooms
2 tablespoons chopped herbs
salt, pepper and a pinch of nutmeg
½ pint red wine
½ pint stock
1 package frozen puff pastry
1 egg

Pre-heat oven to 325°F Mark 3 for meat
Pre-heat oven to 425°F Mark 7 for pastry

Game Pie

Old game birds cooked with bacon and steak and mushrooms in wine, finished with a crust of pastry (Serves 4—6, hot or cold)

1. Cut meat off two grouse (or other game birds), cut steak into small pieces and dice bacon. Arrange in pie dish in layers with finely chopped onion, mushrooms, herbs and seasoning between each layer. Pour over ½ pint red wine and enough stock to barely cover meat. Cover with foil and bake very slowly for 1—1½ hours until all meat is tender. Allow to cool completely.

2. Roll out pastry and place strip around edge of dish, moistened with water. Moisten pastry strip and place a large piece of pastry on top. Press edges together. Cut off surplus and crimp edges. Make slashes in top to release steam and decorate with pastry leaves.

3. Put into oven to bake pastry for about 30 minutes. Serve hot or cold.

Braised Black-cock or Capercaillie

Black-cock or capercaillie braised in red wine sauce with onions, mushrooms, bacon and herbs (Serves 4–5, hot)

1 black-cock or capercaillie 4–6 pounds
4 tablespoons oil
1 oz butter
3 onions
¼ pound mushrooms
2 oz bacon diced
¾ pint red wine
¾–1 pint stock (or more if necessary)
2 tablespoons mixed herbs chopped
1 bay leaf

Pre-heat oven to 350°F Mark 4

1. Heat oil and butter, and brown black-cock or capercaillie all over. Remove to casserole and keep warm. Cook sliced onions, mushrooms and chopped bacon until brown, add red wine and bring to a boil. Set light to wine; when flames die, pour on stock. Add herbs and seasoning. Pour over the bird and cover with lid.

2. Place in oven and cook for 1½ hours, or until tender. Remove from casserole and carve. Place pieces on serving dish. Bring cooking sauce to boil and strain, skim off fat, and serve as gravy.

3. Serve with potatoes or noodles and redcurrant or cranberry jelly.

Roast Quail in Vine Leaves

Quails stuffed with butter and wrapped in vine leaves and bacon, roasted in butter and served on slices of buttered toast chips (Serves 4, hot)

4 quails
2½ oz butter
a squeeze of lemon juice
4 tender vine leaves
4 slices fat bacon
4 slices white bread
fried breadcrumbs

Pre-heat oven to 450°F Mark 8

1. Clean and truss quails neatly. Put ¼ oz butter inside each with lemon juice and salt and pepper. Wrap each one in a vine leaf; then tie a slice of fat bacon around each bird.

2. Heat butter, put quails into roasting pan and baste. Roast in oven for 15 minutes or grill on a spit.

3. Make 4 slices of toast and butter lightly. When birds are cooked, spread toast with pan drippings and serve.

Roast Grouse

Tender young grouse stuffed with butter and seasoning, wrapped in bacon and roasted; served with bread sauce, gravy, and game chips (Serves 4, hot)

2 young grouse
2 oz butter
4 slices fat bacon
¼–½ pint red wine
2 slices bread
¼ pint stock

Pre-heat oven to 425°F Mark 7

1. Put 1 oz butter with seasoning inside each bird. Wrap them in bacon, and roast in oven for 30–35 minutes, until tender. Pour 2 glasses of red wine into pan after about 15 minutes and baste.

2. Make two slices of toast and when birds are done put one on each. Carve each bird in half for serving.

3. Meanwhile, make bread sauce as in *Roast Chicken* (see p. 26) and game chips as in *Roast Pheasant* (see p. 55).

4. Make gravy from pan drippings, adding stock and a little more wine. boil up and serve.

Salmi of Grouse or Partridge

Half cooked game, jointed and simmered in stock and served with thickened sauce (Serves 4–6, hot)

2 grouse or partridges or small guinea fowl
3 tablespoons oil
3–4 rashers streaky bacon
¾ pint strong stock
¼ pint red wine (or port)
½ oz flour
½ oz butter
1 tablespoon parsley chopped

Pre-heat oven to 400°F Mark 6

1. Heat oil in roasting pan, cover birds with bacon and roast in hot fat for 20 minutes. Remove from oven and allow to cool slightly. Carve birds into pieces and put into a casserole. Cover with strong stock, add herbs and seasoning, and cook gently in oven for 15 minutes, or until tender.

2. Remove birds to serving dish and keep warm in oven. Bring pan drippings to the boil and reduce quantity slightly. Add wine (or port) and cook for a few minutes. Thicken sauce with small pieces of butter and flour paste, and continue heating until sauce thickens. Spoon over pieces of game, sprinkle with chopped parsley, and serve.